GABY NATALE

THE VIRTUOUS Circle

Translated by Yalimal Vidal

HARPERCOLLINS
LEADERSHIP

AN IMPRINT OF HARPERCOLLINS

Published by HarperCollins Leadership, an imprint of HarperCollins Focus LLC.

Any internet addresses, phone numbers, or company or product information printed in this book are offered as a resource and are not intended in any way to be or to imply an endorsement by HarperCollins Leadership, nor does HarperCollins Leadership vouch for the existence, content, or services of these sites, phone numbers, companies, or products beyond the life of this book.

ISBN 978-1-4002-2015-1 (eBook)
ISBN 978-1-4002-2010-6 (Paperback)

Library of Congress Control Number: 2020945465

Printed in the United States of America
20 21 22 23 LSC 10 9 8 7 6 5 4 3 2 1

Dedication

To Andy, my great love and companion on life's
adventures for fifteen years. Every turn in *the Virtuous Circle*
is more beautiful because I turn hand in hand with you.

To Roberto, Cristina, Alejandro, and Francisco for
giving me the foundations that allowed me to dream.

To rebel dreamers who dare to see beyond the visible.

Contents

Preface

The *Virtuous* Circle is a book for dreamers, the *rebels at heart* who see beyond the circumstances surrounding them. Those who suspect that something wonderful is waiting for them but have not yet dared to take that first step toward their new destination.

Why is it that some people who seem to have it all never reach their full potential while others born into adversity beat the odds and become the highest, truest versions of themselves?

This is the question that led me to write *The Virtuous Circle* after ten years of interviews with pioneers and superachievers from different disciplines.

Here you will find tools for self-improvement as well as personal stories and testimonies from international trailblazers such as Deepak Chopra and Carlos Santana. Their stories reveal the amazing power of enthusiasm when it comes to transforming lives.

Do you feel like there is a treasure inside you? Are you tired of your fears preventing you from spreading your wings and sharing that treasure with the world? Stop running around in circles ... and get on *the Virtuous Circle!*

Letter to the Reader

Dear Underdog,

This book is my love letter to you.

I SEE YOU.

I see you working twice as hard to get half as far. I see you do more with less. I see you, the one people do not expect to win.

I KNOW YOU.

I know you take a deep breath before entering a room where your individuality is met by a sea of sameness. I know you outwork the rest in hopes that overdelivering will protect you from other people's prejudice. I know you are tired of pushing yourself to prove your worth to skeptics.

I CELEBRATE YOU.

I celebrate your refusal to trade authenticity for acceptance. I celebrate your courage in the face of adversity. I celebrate your appetite to be what you cannot yet see in the world.

YOUR LIFE STORY IS NOT AN APOLOGY.

This book is the story of an underdog who became obsessed with interviewing fellow underdogs to create a roadmap that can help others around the world in the pursuit of their dreams. *The Virtuous Circle* is also the result of my frustration when I could not find books on personal growth written by people like me.

As a Latina who happens to be an immigrant, every time I saw myself represented in media, I felt I was reduced to a stereotype. Tired of seeing how others did an awful job at portraying my rich and multidimensional heritage, I decided it was time to write my own story. Today, I am proud to say I am the first Latina author published by HarperCollins Leadership.

So how do leadership and self-help look if you are an underdog? You are about to find out.

The Virtuous Circle is here to tell you that there is beauty in being an underdog. To remind you that you do not need to change yourself to feel worthy. And that wonderful things can happen even in difficult times.

THE WORLD HAS CHANGED.
THE SELF-HELP SPACE . . . NOT SO MUCH.

I have always had an ambivalent relationship with the self-help world. Personal growth books have always been there for me every time life throws a curveball. But lately, I am seeing some trends in the self-help space that are genuinely concerning.

Way too often, I find myself let down by "leaders" who do not embody the principles they claim to teach. Some brag about possessions, relationships, or credentials that were not true to begin with. Others profited from an image that turned out to be false. A few claimed to be self-made but in reality came from money or married into it.

As someone who is both an author and a reader in this space, I find the lack of accountability frustrating. There are plenty of people who talk the talk. Not that many have the commitment to walk the walk.

As of late, I cannot shake the feeling that the self-help industry is becoming . . . unrelatable.

Not all forms of optimism come from the same place. There is a kind of optimism that is part of the toolkit that some of us need to develop to overcome adversity. *Things will work out. I know it because this is not my first rodeo.* This is the kind of optimism that moves me to the core.

There is another kind of optimism that is quite different. It comes from not having to endure the same hardships others must face. *Things will work out. I know it because they have always worked out for me.*

The first kind of optimism comes from resilience. The second comes from privilege.

Behind every Instagram post that claims "Just Do It. Only You Control Your Life" lies the illusion of a *level playing field*. Refusing to acknowledge that generational poverty, racial inequality, or nepotism play a role in the journey to accomplishment is the very definition of privilege. Only those who were never affected by systemic inequalities can pretend that they do not exist.

No. Everything is *not* just a matter of personal responsibility. There is something cruel about making people feel inadequate for life circumstances they did not choose. It sends the dangerous message that if you did not make it, it was *only* because you did not want it badly enough.

Any underdog knows that the reality is much more complicated. That is why advice coming from privileged optimism sounds tone-deaf to so many of us. Building a positive mindset and addressing negative self-talk are important. But they are only one part of the equation.

THE VIRTUOUS CIRCLE: FROM INDIVIDUAL ACHIEVEMENT TO COLLECTIVE WELLBEING

Here's a message to anyone who wants to make an impact in the world: **The goal should not be to *only* make the best of the cards life has dealt you. The goal should also be to use your achievements for something greater than yourself.**

Let us all contribute to changing the rules.

This is one of the reasons why *The Virtuous Circle* goes beyond individual goal-setting. It aims for collective wellbeing. If there's anything to be learned from the economic, sanitary, environmental, and spiritual crisis we've faced, it is that our selves, our wellbeing, and our future are inextricably linked to the rest of our fellow human beings. Making it big but alone does not solve the problems we have in front of us.

Love,

Gabby Natale

Introduction

MAKING PEACE WITH UNCERTAINTY

Do you know what you are?
You are a manuscript of a divine letter.
You are a mirror reflecting a noble face.
This universe is not outside of you.
Look inside yourself;
everything that you want,
you are already that.

— RUMI

This book began with a small act of bravery that was rewarded by the universe. *The Virtuous Circle* is the result of an incredible chain of events that unleashed a domino effect: events that can be explained only as the work of destiny.

The first domino fell on a rainy winter night. It came in the form of a revelation.

Every December, I like to do an exercise. I close my eyes, reflect on the year that is ending, and visualize the one about to begin. I think about what I can do to make the new year better than the last one. This practice gives me more clarity about what I have experienced and reminds me that I have before me a blank slate on which I can rewrite my story.

As a communicator, I have interviewed hundreds of people, and I know from experience that the best conversations occur when my guests forget the cameras and speak with an open heart. No posing, no scripts. Just brutal honesty. That was exactly how I spoke to myself that day.

As I reflected, I discovered something I didn't like: I realized that in the previous 365 days I had not left my comfort zone. I had, more or less, played it safe. It became clear to me that to continue growing in the following year, I needed to give myself permission to take more risks, to move beyond the known. I needed to do something scary. I had to abandon the role of only asking questions and start finding my own answers. I needed to share my story.

Tick . . . the first domino had fallen, and without knowing it, I was already writing a new chapter of my life.

The days passed and the usual December marathon began: my mother-in-law Marta and my brother Francisco visited. Together, we planned a festive menu of homemade pasta, and then we enjoyed all the celebrations of the season. For a few days I had almost no opportunity to reflect on my revelation.

But on December 21, an email arrived that would test me. Buried among all the end-of-year messages, it announced that this was the last day to enter a contest organized by YouTube called *Storytellers*.

The rules were simple: you had to send in a two-minute video telling a story from your life. The organizers would select five stories, and the winners would have the opportunity to share them in front of a live audience at a conference in Los Angeles.

One more detail caught my attention. The name of the conference was suggestive: #*WeAllGrow*. That was just what I had proposed to do the following year. Could it be a coincidence?

A voice deep inside told me to set aside my doubts and enter the contest. Like an annoying gadfly, it persisted in telling me again and again how great an idea this was.

You have wanted to face a challenge for some time. This is an opportunity to experience something new. This will not be like when you do an interview on the show or host an event. Here there is no preset script or theme of the day. There is no right or wrong content. It's about the story of your life.

While this voice of enthusiasm tried to seduce me, my mind flooded with a thousand reasons why I shouldn't do it.

How ridiculous! Why would a professional journalist share stories about her life that could potentially embarrass her? What could you possibly gain from participating in a contest that isn't even about journalism? What is this business of getting on a stage to talk about my life? If you get nervous and do it wrong, you'll look like a beginner! In five minutes, you'll destroy a reputation that took years to build, and then you'll really have a story to tell!

I spent all day being pulled back and forth between the voices of enthusiasm and fear, which spoke to me in stereo. That night my husband, Andy, and I had dinner reservations to celebrate the fourteenth anniversary of our first kiss.

At 7:30, when I went downstairs to go out, I realized that it was *now or never*. Either I record the video right then and there or I let the opportunity pass me by. I remembered my year-end exercise, and I didn't want fear to decide for me.

So I asked Andy to take my phone and record me. I warned him that I would send whatever was captured in the first take. Without much thought, I spoke for three minutes and sent the video before heading to the restaurant.

Tick . . . the second domino had fallen, and the fate of this book you are reading today was beginning to take shape.

The end-of-year parties went smoothly, and in the first week of January I returned to work after a short break. My work routine returned to normal with meetings, recordings, proposals, and scripts—more or less the usual.

Suddenly, a call interrupted the office hustle and bustle. It was the organizers of the *Storytellers* contest. I had been chosen as one of the winners! What a thrill! In two months, I would be in front of a live audience and would have the opportunity to share part of my life story.

This time I wouldn't go to the safe side. Instead of talking about the red carpets, the celebrities I have interviewed, or the satisfaction I have enjoyed in my career, I decided to go back in time. I made the decision to tell, for the first time and in detail, the story of one of the most vulnerable moments of my life. I would talk about the year and a half I spent unemployed in Argentina just after finishing my studies.

During the following weeks, my backyard became my training ground. Every weekend I sat with my yerba mate tea and a notebook. I wrote down sentences, ideas, and stories I could use for my speech.

The next step was to rehearse out loud. I'm sure that giving an emotional speech to my backyard trees made me look like a good candidate for a psychiatric intervention. Luckily, I have very discreet (or very deaf) neighbors, and they didn't call 911.

The last thing I did before getting on the plane was to take Andy hostage for several hours so he could hear every little last-minute change I had made. Practicing again and again has always made me feel more secure. My husband's a saint and earned his ticket to heaven that day, because when I left, he knew the speech by heart!

While flying to Los Angeles, I didn't suspect that on the other side of the country a mysterious stranger who would leave a mark on my destiny was doing the same. Very soon, our paths would cross.

In Los Angeles, I met the organizers of the event and discovered that *Storytellers* would be the grand finale of the entire #WeAll-Grow conference. It would take place in the largest conference room in the hotel, and they explained that hundreds of people were waiting for this closing event. To top things off, they had assigned me the responsibility of being the first to go onstage. No pressure!

I felt a knot in my stomach.

I want to clarify something here: under normal circumstances, none of this would have been frightening. I have worked in television and performed live events for years. I often host galas and award ceremonies. I have conducted broadcasts, reported news on location, and for ten years I have had my own interview show. But this was different. Unlike all the previous performances, this "news" was my own life. And that changed everything for me.

That night, when I went to sleep, the voice of my fears returned:

Who do you think you are? Why would others want to hear your story? What will your colleagues and your audience think when they know more about your beginnings? You got yourself into this mess. Who told you to open yourself up to ridicule like this for no reason?

My fears were making a desperate last-ditch effort to make me give up. I put the pillow over my head as if I could silence them and fell asleep.

The next day, my fears were back.

Would I be good enough as a speaker? Would my story be interesting enough to connect with the audience? What if my mind went blank and I forgot half the speech?

I showered, reviewed my notes, and practiced the speech a couple more times until it was time to go to the event.

Tick . . . the dominoes of destiny were still falling. That mysterious stranger who had flown coast-to-coast had already arrived. The organizers had invited her, and she would be in the front row at the *Storytellers* gala dinner. Of course, I didn't know all of this, because we hadn't met . . . yet.

I placed the speech notes in my bag and set off for the main event hall. I had to arrive at least one hour before the dinner for a sound check. As I like to be early, I was there about twenty minutes ahead of schedule.

The moment of truth had arrived.

The director asked me to sit at one of the many empty tables in the room and wait a few minutes until they were ready. I realized that it was the first time in many days that I was sitting alone for a few moments, silently and without interruptions.

Instead of reviewing the speech yet again or asking myself for the millionth time how it was going to turn out, I stopped to look around. What I saw amazed me.

To the right, through the large windows, I saw a majestic sunset, the sky dyed pink and imposing over the Pacific Ocean. It was a magical show.

I turned my head to the left and looked around the room, paying attention for the first time. It was beautiful! The stage had a wall with floral arrangements specially prepared for the occasion. Crystal chandeliers refracted the sunlight making small sparkles on the tablecloths. The tables were arranged to perfection. On each plate was a card with a motivational phrase from each of the night's speakers—along with candy. The love and attention to detail the organizers had poured into the event was palpable

Then I realized what was really happening. I had put so much pressure on myself that I was about to experience a wonderful moment . . . and didn't even realize it. I was not "a cow going to the slaughterhouse." On the contrary, I was a tremendously lucky person. I had the great privilege of being able to deliver my message on a stage to an audience that wanted to hear what I had to say.

I relaxed and a great sense of peace flooded over me. All this time I had thought that the speech was a test that I had to pass. I was so foolish!

The speech was not an exam. It was a gift from life.

I thanked God for the opportunity and got carried away by the enthusiasm. I decided that I would fully enjoy every second I was onstage, regardless of the end result. *I no' longer set out to be perfect, only one hundred percent real.*

Tick . . . the most important domino fell into place, and although none of us knew it at that time, this book was beginning to come true. From the front row, paying close attention, a black-eyed stranger watched my every move in silence. Very soon she would make her identity known to me.

I went onstage, opened my heart, and began to share the stories you'll find on these pages.

A Closer Look

Visit www.GabyNatale.com/VirtuousCircle to enjoy the video of #WeAllGrow speech, as well as the audition video my husband recorded with my phone.

CHAPTER 1

WHAT IS THE VIRTUOUS CIRCLE?

#VIRTUOUSCIRCLE

CLOSE YOUR EYES,

open your mind,

AND GIVE YOURSELF
PERMISSION TO SEE
BEYOND THE VISIBLE.

@GABYNATALE

Take a photo and share it online using
#VirtuousCircle

P ut your hand on your heart and honestly ask yourself: How far you could go if you developed your abilities to their full potential?

The only way to know for sure is to start down the path of personal transformation.

The Virtuous Circle teaches you how to use your head and your emotions to defeat the things holding you back. It challenges you to begin the most difficult and satisfying conquest: to conquer yourself.

In *The Virtuous Circle*, you will find practices I learned from pioneers and leaders who have been able to identify, nurture, and manifest their potential. This book includes simple, sequential, and practical steps.

It's not about things magically happening; it's about having a plan that enhances the possibilities that *already live* within you. It's a way of using your intelligence, your thoughts, and your emotions to reach your maximum potential.

I'm convinced that self-improvement is the most valuable asset a person can have in life. And not only is it the most valuable, it's the only one nobody can take away from you. Everything else can vanish without warning: our personal relationships, our material wealth, our health.

Not even the most powerful person on Earth can guarantee they will have one more day of life on this planet. Seeking to control the uncertainty in our lives is a battle we lose before it even begins. The reality is that we have no way of controlling the circumstances that surround us. What we can do is decide how we will react.

HOW WAS THE CONCEPT
FOR THE VIRTUOUS CIRCLE BORN?

One of the things I love most about my profession is that you live a thousand lives in one. I've had the opportunity to live in four countries: the United States, Argentina, Mexico, and England. I've reported from extraordinary places: a morgue in the middle of the desert, the gardens of the White House, an armored Border Patrol car, and the Grammys' red carpet, to name a few.

But what I love most are the people, not the places. For more than ten years, through my television program *SuperLatina*, I have interviewed pioneers who have developed their potential in extraordinary ways.

I've had the chance to meet high-performance athletes, renowned artists, great thinkers, and global leaders. In my program I have learned about paths to success from Deepak Chopra, Carlos Santana, world boxing champions, as well as Emilio Estefan and Enrique Iglesias.

I've also marveled at the stories of anonymous heroes who have survived unimaginable experiences, such as natural catastrophes, human trafficking, or military conflicts. I'm especially fascinated by people who achieve amazing things against all odds. These testimonies, along with my own personal experiences, are the source material for this book.

After years of doing interviews, the idea of *the Virtuous Circle* started to take shape in my head when I asked myself questions that piqued my curiosity.

The first thing I asked myself was: *Is there a quality common to all the extraordinary people I have met and interviewed?*

The answer is *yes*.

Despite having different styles, ages, professions, nationalities, and stories, there is an invisible thread that ties together all those I've interviewed. These headliners and anonymous heroes have cultivated a remarkable quality that distinguishes them from the rest: *they have the ability to see beyond what's visible.*

Consciously or unconsciously, they have allowed themselves to see their beings not only as they are but as they could become. Then they went a step further to find a way to turn that vision into reality.

Now that I had discovered the common thread in the success of so many extraordinary people, I wanted to know more: *Is it possible to group these common elements and synthesize them in a framework of step-by-step action that others can replicate?*

Again, the answer is *yes!* And you will find that framework in *The Virtuous Circle.* You will learn to visualize, plan, execute, perfect, persevere, achieve, inspire, and reach your potential through the seven archetypes that make up *the Virtuous Circle.*

Your first turn in *the Virtuous Circle* is about to begin. Get ready to enjoy every twist along the way. The instructions for this ride are simple and powerful.

The Virtuous Circle is made up of seven archetypes that live within each one of us. Each constitutes a phase and corresponds to a particular action. The seven archetypes and their respective actions are: *the dreamer* (visualize), *the architect* (plan), *the maker* (execute), *the apprentice* (perfect), *the warrior* (persevere), *the champion* (achieve), and *the leader* (inspire).

1. The Dreamer: The dreamer's stage is one of thought and visualization. It begins with imagining something not yet present in reality. It's the spark that begins *the Virtuous Circle.*

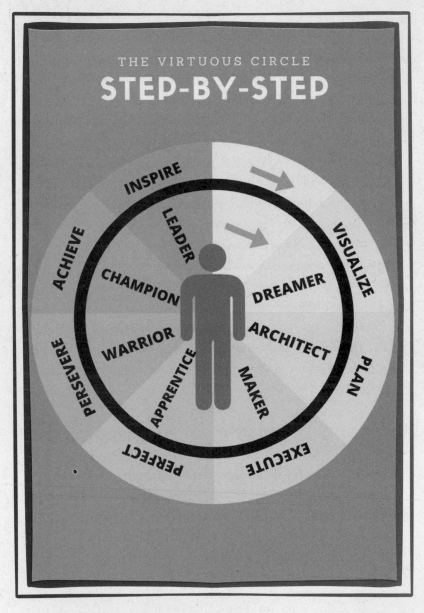

The Virtuous Circle: seven archetypes that go from idea to execution.

This is the time to connect with the essence of our inner child, that same child who danced happily and carelessly, not wondering what the right steps were, not caring if someone else had better rhythm. This stage is an opportunity to begin to unlearn external conditioning and abandon self-limiting thoughts in order to let our minds fly and see beyond the visible.

2. The Architect: In this phase, the architect builds an action map with the ideas and concepts created in the dreamer's stage. It's time to make plans, evaluate options, and analyze what may be the best ways to turn our visions into action.

3. The Maker: This is when theory and reality meet. The architect's plan is put into practice. This is the stage in which the world may reflect back at us the unexpected: the challenges may be greater or different from those we anticipated, the skills we have may not be sufficient, or we may underestimate the time it takes to achieve our dream. We may realize that sometimes even the most "perfect" plans end up being "ferpect" and we will need to reassess.

4. The Apprentice: It's time to focus on perfecting your craft. The apprentice stage represents us following our internal GPS, which asks us to recalculate our route so we can continue moving forward. Now that we've seen our ideas in action, it's time to adjust. In the maker stage, we saw what happens when we put into action all the plans and ideas of the architect and the dreamer. Now is the time for the apprentice to begin the quest for excellence along a path that will eventually lead to mastery. What talents need polishing? What abilities are missing? What strategies work and which ones need to be changed?

5. The Warrior: This is the stage in which our commitment to our dreams is put to the test. In the apprentice stage we perfected our skills and adjusted the action plan. Now is the time to strengthen our tenacity and resilience. We have the skills we need to achieve our goals, but the opportunity we dreamed of has not arrived yet. Frustration and the feelings of injustice lurk close by. We are sorely tempted to abandon our dreams. Now's the time for the brave, for the bold, and for those who keep going when others stop. We have reached the last mile, but we still don't know it—and we constantly wonder if it's worth so much effort. This is the stage when we learn that it takes a true warrior to keep the dream alive.

6. The Champion: All the preparation and work of the previous stages finally meet the opportunity we've been waiting for. It's a time for praise, successes, and applause. But beware of success. Not all that glitters is gold. After achieving their dreams, champions can lose their way. They may give in to new temptations and become a magnet for the wrong type of people.

7. The Leader: This is when the champion becomes an inspiration. Champions achieve their goals. Leaders go one step further by transforming their achievements into something bigger than themselves. The leader not only triumphs but leads by example. Not all champions are leaders, but all leaders are champions.

Before I explain each archetype in detail, I want to make some clarifications about the nature of *the Virtuous Circle*.

The Virtuous Circle is not . . .

Magic: It's not about waving a wand over your life so that solutions magically rain from the sky. Nor is it a recipe to become a millionaire overnight. *The Virtuous Circle* is not part of any religion or sect. It simply represents a way to use your thoughts to work in your favor. It asks you to commit yourself to your dreams and to be a person of action.

The Virtuous Circle is . . .

Sequential: The archetypes that make up *the Virtuous Circle* follow one another. As we move from one archetype to another, our skills and challenges change. Some people will blow past some of these stages while others linger. Furthermore, it is important to know that every time we go from one stage to the next we bring with us the elements and lessons from the phases we leave behind. To become a leader, the person who travels through *the Virtuous Circle* must first have been a champion, a warrior, an apprentice, a maker, an architect, and a dreamer.

Infinite: Upon reaching the last archetype (the leader), *the Virtuous Circle* begins again. It goes from being a Virtuous Circle to becoming a Virtuous Spiral upward. Why do we start over? Because life constantly evolves. Our passage through this world is, like a work of art, never complete but always evolving. Reaching a goal is not the end. We are always starting over. The whole process is restarted with the next skill, idea, project, or task you want to develop. While we are alive, the wheel of experience never stops turning. That's why you can't forget to enjoy every twist and turn *the Virtuous Circle* offers you. Remember that each ending is just a new beginning for the next turn of the Virtuous Spiral that is your life.

Contagious: When *the Virtuous Circle* deeply affects one area of our lives, other areas may also benefit. For example, if *the Virtuous Circle* enables you to improve your health and shed bad habits, surely there will be other areas that will also be affected in a positive way: in the workplace you will have more energy to succeed and advance, in your social life the friends who encourage bad habits will no longer have a place, and so on.

WHAT CAN I USE
THE VIRTUOUS CIRCLE FOR?

It's possible to use *the Virtuous Circle* in any way you choose.

It can be your tool to achieve great transformations, or to reach small goals that have been lingering, those you have not yet been able to conquer. For some, it will be the vehicle that motivates them to get rid of the last five extra pounds. For others, it will be the road map to reinvent themselves and choose a new profession, start a business, develop a new skill, or face a situation that frightens them.

In the next chapters, we will explore in detail the different phases. You will see what each one consists of, what activity defines it, and how it can help you move toward your dream.

In each chapter you will find some practical suggestions to nurture these archetypes in your day-to-day life. I have also created a section called "In the First Person," where I share stories about my own experiences along *the Virtuous Circle*.

In segments called "A Voice of Authority," I include interviews with headliners who have shared their own paths to success with me over the years. The testimonies you will find in these segments include those of Deepak Chopra, Carlos Santana, Isabel Allende, and other great leaders from different fields.

If you want more after reading a chapter, look for the "A Closer Look" box. There you will find my recommendations for additional information or content online.

THE *ENSŌ*: WHAT DOES THE SYMBOL OF *THE VIRTUOUS CIRCLE* MEAN?

The *ensō* is one of the most traditional symbols of Japanese calligraphy. When I saw it, I knew it would be the symbol of *The Virtuous Circle*.

It represents the cycles, repetitions, and the constant movement that governs life and the universe. Drawn with an opening, it reminds us that we are part of something bigger. It also refers to the beauty of imperfection.

In ancient times, Eastern monks entered into a state of meditation to create the *ensō*. They let themselves be guided by their intuition in front of blank pieces of paper and waited for the "perfect moment" to draw the *ensō* in one stroke.

The truth is that like our fingerprints, each *ensō* is unique and unrepeatable. The people who draw them see in them the reflection of the lived moment and of our true being.

● ● ●

A CLOSER LOOK

Visit www.GabyNatale.com/VirtuousCircle and enjoy:

- Personality test: Which of the archetypes of the Virtuous Circle (dreamer, architect, maker, apprentice, warrior, champion, or leader) define you the most?

CHAPTER 2

THE DREAMER: VISUALIZE YOUR DREAM

The secret of genius is to carry the spirit of the child into old age, which means never losing your enthusiasm.

—ALDOUS HUXLEY

#VirtuousCircle

TURN

Enthusiasm

INTO YOUR

COMPASS.

@GabyNatale

 Take a photo and share it online using #VirtuousCircle

T he dreamer is the archetype that kicks off *the Virtuous Circle*. With the dreamer the wheel of personal transformation starts to turn. The dreamer immerses you in the world of ideas and asks you to begin seeing beyond the visible.

But the dreamer is not new to your life. You already know the dreamer.

If you go back in time, you'll remember: you and the dreamer were close friends. You have known each other from when the future was made up of pure possibility. It was a time when you didn't feel ridiculous shouting into the wind that one day you would be a painter, an astronaut, a firefighter, a rock star, or the inventor of a vaccine that would help humanity. No dream seemed too big or eccentric.

You were a child. Your mind didn't question your desires or label them delusional. In your heart, there were only feelings, not calculations. You didn't know if you were going to receive a million-dollar salary for your work or how many sacrifices you would have to make along the way to your dream.

It was incredibly easy to imagine making these dreams come true: three puppets sitting in your room transformed into students in a class where you were the teacher; your old toy car was magically turned into a brand-new race car you drove at full speed; the bathroom mirror became the dressing room vanity of an actress getting ready to debut—with the help of your mom's lipstick.

Those visions of yourself were a genuine result of your enthusiasm. They represented the expression of your dreamer self in its purest form. At this stage of great ingenuity, you didn't know all the many social mandates that would pressure you. Nor did you know the family expectations that would have to be met. You certainly didn't know about the school exams that would label you as "good at this" and "bad at that." All that would come later.

THE LITTLE SHOWGIRL'S DREAM

When I was just a child, I was asked what I wanted to be when I grew up. I would tell anyone who wanted to know that my dream was to be a showgirl. I was fascinated with the lead actresses on variety shows. The beautiful and charismatic women who spent their days dancing, singing, and acting. To me they were dreamlike fairies with their sequin costumes and glamorous style.

The day I graduated from preschool there was a small ceremony in my school's auditorium. When I went onstage to receive my diploma, seeing myself there in front of the audience, I decided to do the same thing showgirls did at the end of the show. I leaned my body and head forward the same way performers do during their final bow. I was ecstatic to greet all my fans from the stage!

There was silence followed by a couple of laughs. Then the school principal made a joke, something like "we have a future actress over here." When I got off the stage, my parents welcomed me, both amused and embarrassed by my childhood antics.

I was only five years old, but even today I remember the ecstasy of my first onstage greeting. It's my earliest memory of connecting with my dreamer self.

As I grew older, real-world responsibilities began to come into my life and my interests changed. I had to study to pass my exams, there were family commitments, and soon I discovered that my musical talent was very limited. There would be no future for me at the *Moulin Rouge* in Paris or dancing the cancan on any variety show!

With the passage of time, my dream of being a showgirl vanished. But the burning desire to pursue a dream has stayed with me forever. My dreamer self planted that seed inside me. To this day I treasure my first time onstage and the intense feeling of being alive that came from greeting my preschool graduation audience.

There is something unprejudiced about being a child that makes the dreamer come forth without fear and allows our fantasies to be freer than at any other time. At age five, I didn't wonder how much money showgirls earned or how hard it would be to get that job. I never even considered if I had the talent—or connections—to do it. I simply let myself be carried away by a dream without judging it, demanding it be practical, or expecting others to validate it.

That dreamer self that we discovered in its purest state when were children still lives inside of us. It doesn't die when we grow up. Sometimes it's hidden and its voice is not heard. Your dreamer self tries to speak to you, but over time it falls on deaf ears. As we got older, the voices of logic told it to shut up! They labeled it crazy. They accused it of living in an unreal world and seeking impossible goals. But your dreamer self is still there. Seek it. Claim it!

The dreamer is the one who reminds you that life is an adventure worth exploring and that being an adult is no excuse to numb your curiosity. It invites you to try new things, expand your horizons, and let your imagination fly. The dreamer pushes you to believe more in yourself and your ideas, even when you still don't have visible results that validate your vision. The dreamer invites you to flee the conventional and gives you permission to play and reinvent yourself. It accompanies you every time you sing loudly in the car and winks when you lose your inhibitions and have fun at a costume party.

Recovering your dreamer self is not about becoming Peter Pan, forgetting responsibilities and throwing everything away. It's about reconnecting with that feeling of enthusiasm and unlimited possibility you had as a child.

Now, close your eyes and remember. Search for that dreamer self that still lives in you. Borrow from it the clarity to rethink your dreams without prejudice.

Sometimes, to go forward in the direction of your dreams, you need to first take a look back.

Something to Think About

- *What is your first memory about your dreamer self?*
- *What would happen in your life today if you could recover that feeling of unlimited possibility you had while you were a child?*
- *What changes would you make in your life if you felt the same courage you had in your childhood, when you dreamed without judging your dreams?*
- *What "truths" of the world would you challenge if you felt as invincible as when you were a child?*

PLANTING DREAMS:
THE DREAMER AND FREEDOM

The dreamer is your greatest ally when you dive deep into your being, start to see beyond the visible, and take a turn on *the Virtuous Circle*. With the dreamer, you have the opportunity to develop a new consciousness: to see yourself through the eyes of pure potential. The dreamer will help you appreciate yourself based not only on who you are today but on who you can become if you develop to the fullest the gifts that you *already* have inside you, the gifts that now lie dormant.

Part of your job at this stage is to create the conditions necessary for your dreamer self to flourish.

A mind plagued with social conditioning, tormented by an end-less parade of fears, or devoid of enthusiasm is hardly the fertile ground you need to sow your most intimate desires. To create that fertile field, you have to isolate that "emotional noise," like separat-ing the wheat from the chaff.

The dreamer in you has a request: that your dream be an au-thentic celebration of your individuality. The wings to develop your highest being are large and powerful, but they can only spread in all their splendor if your dream is a genuine expression of who you are. There is no greatness in spending your life imi-tating others or in dedicating your existence to meeting someone else's expectations.

THE ONLY WAY TO HONOR YOUR
DESTINY IS TO WALK YOUR OWN PATH.

Ask your dreamer self to help you start this journey down the path to self-discovery. What's that thing that makes you feel excited and allows you to make your light shine? We all have a way of doing something that nobody else can copy. The key is to discover what it is and embrace it with the dreamer's contagious energy.

This task is a huge responsibility. No one can do it for you. Those around you, even if they love you and wish you well, can't walk a mile in your shoes. They can't live in your skin for a day and find out what gives you pleasure and what brings you tre-mendous pain. In his magnificent 1859 essay "On Liberty," English philosopher John Stuart Mill argues that liberty is a precondition for happiness, drawing a clear boundary between those who decide their destiny and those who do not:

> *He who lets the world, or his own portion of it, choose his plan of life for him, has no need of any other faculty than the ape-like one of imitation. He who chooses his plan for himself, employs all his faculties. He must use observation to see, reasoning and judgment to foresee, activity to gather materials for decision, discrimination to decide, and when he has decided, firmness and self-control to hold to his deliberate decision.*[1]

Exercising free will is a difficult task, but one can only dream of true freedom when we make the courageous decision to face doubts, fears, mandates, and insecurities in the pursuit of our own happiness.

Questions asked by those who follow the dreams of others:

- What do people in my position and status generally do?
- What should I be doing now according to my age, profession, etc.?
- What are the achievements that would make my parents/children/friends/partner happier?
- What are the things you would have to do/achieve/buy to impress others?

Questions from your dreamer self to help you visualize your own dream:

- What are the interests, abilities, or preferences that make me unique and unrepeatable?

- What activities make me profoundly happy?
- What professions or occupations are compatible with my personality?
- What decisions would promote the development of my higher self?
- What skills that make me happy can make a positive impact when used to serve others?

WHAT SPIRITUAL FUEL ARE YOU USING TO MOVE ALONG THE VIRTUOUS CIRCLE?

In the world there is more and more talk about the types of energy we use. Some, such as wind and solar, are considered cleaner for the planet because they are renewable and less harmful.

At the other extreme are the toxic, nonrenewable fuels of oil, coal, and natural gas. These pollute the air, contaminate the oceans, and can be poison you if breathe their fumes. Not to mention, they are considered responsible for climate change.

In the same way, there are different types of fuels for our spirit. Some energy sources are purer than others. That's why it's important that in addition to thinking about your dream, you take time to reflect on what is the motivation or "fuel" behind that dream.

What source of energy will you use to move along the road? Depending on how your spiritual fuel originates, it can be reactive or active.

Reactive spiritual fuels. These impure energies connect you to negative feelings such as envy, hatred, or resentment. By definition, they arise in response to external stimuli. For example, a grudge against someone who harmed you. They may also take the form of an obsessive competitiveness to show how capable you are to someone who did not believe in you. Or perhaps, they can manifest as the tempting idea to "teach a lesson" to someone who has tricked you.

Who hasn't fantasized about a cheating ex squirming in regret when they find us happily getting on with our lives?

We are human, and revenge fantasies can be comforting in a moment of vulnerability. But you must be careful not to fuel your dreams with this kind of energy. If you base your success on narcissism, obsessive competition, or envy, you will become a bottomless barrel that no success will ever be enough to satisfy. Make sure that the motivation for your dream is always your own development and not the detriment of others.

Some people have come a long way using impure spiritual fuels; they have built their success on lies, envy, and taking all kinds of moral shortcuts. The problem with impure spiritual fuels is not that they're inefficient but that they're despicable. They also make you pay a heavy price. Those bad feelings are like a boomerang that sooner or later returns to you. Or worse, they return for your health.

If you use impure spiritual fuels, you will never be free. Even if you achieve everything you set your mind to, you will remain enslaved because you will always be looking over your shoulder. So every time you feel tempted to use impure energy to go further on your path, remember this saying: "Before you embark on a journey of revenge, dig two graves."

Active spiritual fuels. These pure energies connect you to the best parts of yourself. They make you want to move forward simply to improve yourself, to help others with your knowledge or talent, or because you are genuinely happy perfecting a skill.

The irrefutable proof that you are using pure energies is that as you travel the road, you become a better person moment by moment. You will feel more comfortable in your own skin and more grateful for every step you take. You will want to give the world some of what it has given you. If you feel optimistic and full of energy, if time flies when you're doing what you chose, those are signs you are on the right track.

Something to Think About

If you still don't know what your dream is, use your heart as a compass. What things make you feel fulfilled, useful, free, full of love, and enthusiastic?

VISUALIZE:
THE ART OF BELIEVING THEN SEEING

The clothes that cover you, the roof that protects you, the books and movies that entertain you, the laws that govern your city or country: all things, absolutely all of them, first began as an idea! Someone initially conceived of them, and only after that did they become something real.

Many of the things we take for granted today, such as robotics or women's right to vote, seemed like impossible ideas when they were conceived. But time, talent, and hard work made them a reality.

This is why, instead of "seeing is believing" as the saying goes, you have to give yourself permission to believe . . . even before seeing! Humanity's greatest innovations are the products of people who had the ability to think that something never seen before could not only be imagined but also built.

And even if your dream is not to create the most powerful computer on the planet or design a spacecraft that will travel to an unknown galaxy, you need to use the same guiding principle as the greatest inventors in the history of humankind: *you must allow yourself to see beyond the visible.*

Start by paying special attention to your thoughts. How is your internal dialogue? What are you telling yourself? Are you empowering—or sabotaging—yourself with the messages you send? Remember that those thoughts are the seeds of the reality that you want to create for your future.

The dreamer teaches us that the first step to living our dream is to learn the art of visualization.

But . . . what is visualization?

To visualize is to use your imagination to create mental images.

It starts with closing your eyes and imagining what you want to experience in your reality. In your mind you can create a film of the life you want for yourself. The more details you can imagine, the better!

In the most difficult moments of my life, I have held on to my visualizations so tightly that I could have won an Oscar for Best Director of Mental Films.

Making visualization a regular habit will keep you focused on your dream. This is a fundamental exercise, because thoughts have great power over us. We become what we think about all day.

One of the most important things to do as you close your eyes and begin to visualize your future is to watch out for the process of your own thinking, your assumptions, your thought patterns. Make a conscious effort to always come from a place of abundance.

Know that within yourself there is a universe of possibilities available to you. Don't be afraid to create something in your mind that has not yet happened for you, your family, your creed, nation, or place of origin.

Don't let your dream of tomorrow be conditioned by the events of yesterday. Don't let the frustrations of others affect your dream either—those who longed for something but didn't get it and now say what you want is impossible too. Past events and others' experiences can't predict your future possibilities.

We can use visualization as an exercise to gradually develop a greater understanding of ourselves. Some visualizations will flow freely. But some aren't so easy to project onto our psyches.

In this exercise, you may discover that to dream big you have to face your own fears. Take note if a dream is especially difficult to visualize. Perhaps some emotional blockage or self-limiting thought lurks behind it.

In my case, for example, I had to reprogram my thoughts about money and prosperity. I realized that I had grown up suspicious of those who had accumulated great personal wealth. This revelation became clear when I emigrated to the United States from Argentina at twenty-three.

In Argentina, society is generally suspicious of people who have amassed a fortune. Sadly, this suspicion is justified by the almost daily discoveries of corruption. So even without being aware of it, I had distrusted those who managed to have a robust bank account.

In the United States, people have the opposite attitude. People who have managed to become wealthy are generally admired and celebrated.

When I emigrated, I held two strongly contrasting points of view—the inherited and the new. I realized my own prejudices and why it was so difficult for me to visualize anything that had to do with material abundance. How could I imagine myself surrounded by prosperity if I was unconsciously labeling as "suspicious" those who had managed to amass a fortune?

I'm sharing this experience because I know that when you start visualizing your dream you will come face-to-face with your own prejudices. The more resistant you are to imagining some aspect of your dream, the more likely it is that you have an emotional block in that area.

Making progress and experiencing setbacks is normal. Even the most confident person has self-limiting thoughts hidden somewhere. When you encounter barriers in your visualization, don't be angry with yourself. Use it as an opportunity to reflect and to ask yourself why this is happening to you.

Examples of self-limiting thoughts:

About work and money . . .

- Wealthy people are not good. They must have made their money dishonestly.
- If someone has money, it's because they took it from others. For someone to have more money, another person must have less.
- Success is achieved only if we suffer along the way. To achieve success, the price to be paid is happiness.
- All successful people believe themselves to be superior to others. Don't go near them, because they will want to humiliate you.

About love and partners . . .

- Nobody likes to go on a date with people as independent/chubby/young/old/conservative/liberal/ etc. as me.

- All worthwhile people are already in a relationship.
- You can't have everything. If I'm lucky in love, I won't be lucky at work, in health, or in some other area of my life.

About health issues . . .
- Addictions run in my family. If my father/mother/ brother/etc. was an addict, I will be too. It's my destiny.
- All my life I have been overweight. The diets and treatments I followed always failed. It's clear that I must resign myself to failure. I can never improve my fitness.
- My family history includes mental illnesses. With these genes I'm doomed to suffer depression/schizophrenia/ suicidal thoughts/etc.

SOME PRACTICAL SUGGESTIONS TO FEED THE DREAMER IN YOU

- *If you want to move faster, look for stillness.* To say that having moments of stillness will make you go faster seems like a contradiction, but it's not. If you reserve a few minutes a day to remain silent with yourself, you will have invested a small part of your day to receive something important: greater clarity. Dreamers need to have a mental space to identify their own emotions. In this phase of *the Virtuous Circle* you are building the mental foundations for everything that will come later. It's important to be able to determine if the path you're dreaming of excites you, to discover if some thought is sabotaging you, and to know what kind of "spiritual fuel" is powering your dream.

That silent time with ourselves is tremendously important. Some people spend their silent time drawing. Others prefer meditating. And some prefer to go for a walk to clear their minds. There is no formula perfect for everyone. Choose the one that best suits your personality and lifestyle. You can do it!

• *Create your dream map of the Virtuous Circle.* One way to motivate yourself and have your dream always in sight is to create a dream map. Dream maps are collage-like visual expressions where you collect images of what you would like to attract into your life.

There are many ways to do it. You can even create your dream map using *the Virtuous Circle* diagram as a step-by-step guide to visualize the stages of your transformation. To do this, take a blank sheet and draw a circle. Then divide it into seven slices. Each one will contain a stage of *the Virtuous Circle* (dreamer, architect, maker, apprentice, warrior, champion, and leader). In the center you can place your photo or draw a silhouette that identifies you. Then, using magazine images, personal photos, memories, and motivational phrases, fill each section.

If, for example, you need to learn to play the guitar to make your dream come true, you can add a picture of the guitar you'd like to use in your lessons. If your leader stage includes sharing your message with others through teaching, special trips, or a book, those images should go there. The idea is that your circle is full of inspiration!

Another way to make the dream map is to divide the circle into different areas of your life (work, health and well-being, love, etc.) and then cut out the images that correspond to each of those.

For example, if you want more balance between your personal life and your work life, cut out images of the personal interests that you would like to pursue. When you have your dream map finished, hang it in a very visible place. Make sure it's the first thing you see in the morning and the last thing you see before going to sleep. Having your dream always in sight is very powerful.

- *Turn enthusiasm into your compass.* The word *enthusiasm* comes from the Greek *entheos,* which means "to have a God within one's self." An enthusiastic person is someone guided by divine strength and wisdom. Someone who has the joy of enthusiasm is, in a certain way, experiencing a connection with the most sacred part of themselves.

  During a speech at Stanford University in 2005, Steve Jobs shared an exercise he did every morning to measure his enthusiasm. When he looked in the mirror, he asked himself: *If today were the last day of my life, would I like to do what I am going to do today?* If the answer was no for too many days in a row, he knew he needed to change something.

  Enthusiasm is that divine spark that will serve you as a compass when you are lost. What would happen to artists, innovators, and all those who seek excellence in their fields if there were no enthusiasm?

- *Connect with other dreamers.* Think about the people around you. Are there any dreamers in your circle of family or friends? It doesn't have to be someone who shares the same dream as you. It can be those who simply inspire commitment, creativity, or a positive attitude. These dreamers may have succeeded in something you're not interested in; but you and them see the world beyond the visible. If they are approachable, contact them. Ask them to tell you about their own paths to success.

Take advantage of the opportunities that the Internet gives you. Look for communities of like-minded people. If your dream is to complete a marathon, look for web pages for marathoners. Find social media groups where runners meet. Get information on the right shoes and the best marathons. Learn everything that has to do with your dream. The more you begin to relate to that world, the more excited you will get and the more detailed your dream visualizations will become.

In the First Person

An Unemployed Woman in Argentina Dares to Dream

The kettle was whistling and I thought it would be a good idea to drink something hot. As I got up from my chair, I realized that my legs had fallen asleep. How many hours had I spent sitting in front of the computer in the same position? I hobbled to the kitchen and poured hot water into a cup.

While sweetening the tea, I mentally reviewed the results of my job search. Resumes Sent: 117; Answers Obtained: 40; Job Interviews: 0.

It was still the age of dial-up Internet, so I disconnected from the network to free up the phone line and check my voicemail box. I hoped that some human resources department in one of the many companies I had called had left me a message. But my voicemail box was empty.

Either way, it would be another day of sending lots of resumes and getting no results. Sometimes I wondered why I had studied for so many years if at the end of the day my diplomas failed to open any doors.

I went to the bathroom and washed my face. I glanced at the mirror and stared at my reflection: I had been wearing the same blue shirt for two days. I paused on my hair. It seemed to belong to two different heads: one half was straight, and the other half bulged with bedhead.

As I walked back to the computer, I looked down. Surprise! I was wearing different colored socks. "Now I'm ready for the runway," I said to myself.

I remembered that Andy, my boyfriend (now my husband), was in the next room, and I felt guilty. I was embarrassed to let him see me like this. When we met, I was always put together, but now I looked pulled apart. The glamazon he once knew had turned—at best—into a plain Jane. For a moment I thought about taking out my curling iron, but I really didn't have the strength to fix myself up.

Then the television caught my attention. My favorite afternoon talk show was starting. It was the type of show that mixes the news with celebrity interviews and inspirational stories. On the screen, the host made her triumphant entry. I was mesmerized, so I decided to take a break to clear my head.

For me, television has always been a passport to a dream world. I'm cheesy, I know. The disappointments of young love could be healed between heavy sighs as love stories played out in soap operas. A bad day at school could be forgotten as I ate toast and enjoyed the twists and turns of a comedy. And even a simple winter scarf could be magically transformed into an exquisite feather boa as I danced in my pajamas to music videos. I was so fascinated by everything about that little box. It was irresistible to me!

The magical world of television contained a disturbing duality: it was both immediate and inaccessible. It was so close that it became a reality at the push of a button, but it was as far away as the moon because I didn't know anyone who worked there.

My parents always made very clear to me that the captivating world of rainbow confetti television offered was not for girls like me. Everyone knows that the studious daughters of lawyers only work in "respectable" places like embassies, banks, consulting companies, or multinational corporations. It was well known that television sets were intended for indecent women! How many times had they told me? Apparently not enough because my fascination with television survived.

In that afternoon talk show, the time had come for the thought of the day. It seemed like the message was custom made for me. "Make yourself a priority," the larger than life television host exclaimed with unmatched charisma. "If you are lying in bed feeling sad, don't allow it. If you are angry, hit a pillow, but don't let yourself falter. Do something for your life . . . now!"

The more I listened to her, the more magnetic she seemed to me. It had been a while since she had turned fifty and she wasn't especially beautiful, but she had something that I didn't have at that moment: confidence. It was as if the cameras had given her superpowers. I came to think that it was impossible for this woman to stutter or make mistakes. She felt like the queen of television!

She had a quality that only good presenters have: she made you forget your problems. Watching the show, you immersed yourself in her world. And in doing so, you too felt a little invincible.

I was so absorbed with the show that I barely noticed Andy had left the room and was passing behind me. When I saw him, I turned around and without thinking said with enthusiasm: "Look at this woman, for God's sake. It must be amazing to be able to host your own television show! In my next life I want to host one too!"

Andy got serious. He took my face in his hands gently and looked into my eyes. Then he asked me firmly: "Why are you going to wait until your next life?"

There was silence. I didn't know what to say. Instead, I cried like a little girl.

That question changed my life.

Without realizing it, I had assumed that something that could make me so very happy, like having my own show, was absolutely beyond my reach. Discouragement had so numbed my soul that I had not even given myself permission to dream.

If I never tried, how could I be sure that I would never be able to host a television program? For the first time, I was aware of my own self-limiting thoughts. It was crazy! I was only twenty-three years old. I had my whole life ahead of me, and without realizing it I was already starting to throw in the towel. It was like a football player giving up on the championship before even going out on the field.

I decided to treasure Andy's question in my heart—"Why are you going to wait until your next life?"—and I've dusted it off every time I was afraid to do something that excited me. This experience taught me a great lesson I always remember when I go through difficult times:

WE MUST NOT JUMP TO PERMANENT CONCLUSIONS BASED ON TEMPORARY CIRCUMSTANCES.

It's true that my reality at that time was not easy. I probably had valid reasons to feel discouraged. Not getting a job is unpleasant. But one thing was clear: unemployment was not an irreversible fact. And that made all the difference.

My mistake had been to make *permanent conclusions* about my possibilities ("I won't be able to have my own television show") based on *temporary circumstances* (unemployment). This is one of the most common mistakes of those who abandon their dreams prematurely.

Luckily, Andy had the clarity that I lacked in that moment of weakness. He believed in me and saw potential I had not yet discovered in myself. That is why I believe that being surrounded by allies is fundamental to our life and personal development. Our allies are like angels that lift us up when we feel we no longer have strength . . . and we all have those moments from time to time.

Something to Think About

My "permanent conclusion" in the face of a temporary circumstance was to mistakenly assume that I would never be able to work on camera in a television show. What is yours?

A Voice of Authority

The Dreamer—Carlos Santana

"YOU ARE ALREADY WHAT YOU WANT TO BECOME; IT'S THE OTHERS WHO DON'T KNOW IT."

Carlos Santana is a *supernatural* man, just like the name of his famous album. I'm not just saying that because of the

Photo with Carlos Santana in his personal studio in Las Vegas.

supernatural musical talent that has earned him ten Grammy awards, a star on the Hollywood Walk of Fame, and thirty million records sold around the planet, but also because Carlos Santana's arrival into the world was somehow supernatural.

Few know it, but Carlos was a baby who shouldn't have been born. His own father, José Santana, ordered that he be aborted.

The story goes that when Carlos's father found out that his wife was pregnant, the news was not well received. Mr. Santana was convinced that four children were more than enough for this humble family from Autlán, Mexico. A fifth child would only deepen the financial problems that already troubled them.

Mr. Santana decided to act. He gave his wife a firm order to drink a special herbal tea designed to terminate the pregnancy. An unexpected twist of fate would ruin his plan, however, and save little Carlos.

Chepa, the maid, was the one in charge of preparing the powerful abortive concoction. "Boil this thing. I want to see that my wife drinks it all," Mr. Santana told the maid. What Mr. Santana didn't know is that the pious Chepa would disobey her employer's order and prepare the mixture by replacing the powerful abortive tea with a simple regular one. Months later, Carlos was born.

Perhaps it's because he's inspired by his own story that Carlos jokingly tells young musicians, "Just relax. You already passed the audition. You were born!" That ability to tell stories about his painful moments and transform them into lessons endeared me when I finally met Carlos.

For the interview, he invited me to his private rehearsal room in Las Vegas. One of the first things I noticed was the simplicity of his offices, even though they were in Sin City, a town of luxurious excess.

There was no fancy furniture. No giant posters of him on every wall. No entourage of half-terrified people typical of the big stars. If it weren't for the vintage guitars on the walls, nothing would indicate that this is the creative space of a man who has had his fingers on the pulse of music for five decades.

Before our interview, Carlos made a single request to his assistants: he wanted them to light incense to perfume the room. He does this in his hotel rooms too. It's his way of transforming any room, anywhere on the planet into a familiar place. And so, between incense and guitars, the interview began.

Gaby: When did you realize you had talent? In retrospect it must be easy to pinpoint, but, were you aware of your own potential when you were struggling the most?

Carlos: I knew that I had enough tenacity to become someone like B. B. King or Tito Puente. Or that I would become who I am now. It was other people who didn't know it! That is what you have to tell yourself. They ask me: "What advice would you give young people?" And I don't want to tell them what to do or how to do things. However, I want to assure them of something: *you are already what you want to become; it's the others who don't know it.* You must visualize what you will be doing in five years, including how much money you want to earn and how you want to live. If you don't believe in yourself, who else will believe in you?

Here is something beautiful to reflect on: there is a difference between supreme conviction and arrogance. Arrogance is fear. Supreme conviction is light, not fear. You know what you want, you need it, you want to get it.

Gaby: Speaking of convictions, you have said that you are convinced that you came into the world because an angel intervened. Otherwise, your life would have ended before birth.

Carlos: Exactly. But that was one of the many golden opportunities with which I've been blessed. We all have saints, angels, or archangels that will appear in our lives at the right time to help us. I don't believe in coincidences or good luck. I live in Las Vegas, but I don't believe in luck! I believe in the grace of God; it's guaranteed to flow.

Carlos is not one of those interviewees who goes on autopilot. He is the type who takes a moment to reflect, and then he shares his inner world with each answer. He knows that it takes a brave soul to be vulnerable.

It's precisely that spiritual strength that prevented him from falling apart during the most painful moments.

Life put Carlos to the test at a very young age. When he was just a ten-year-old boy, a family friend took advantage of and sexually abused him. Embarrassed, Santana kept this dark secret buried deep within. It took five decades and intense therapy for him to heal his heart and feel ready to share this incident with his audience. He decided to talk about his nightmare because he wanted to transform it into a healing balm that would help others. Finally, he had achieved the unimaginable: to forgive the man who stole his innocence.

Gaby: Let's talk about your revelation that you were a victim of sexual abuse during your childhood. In a macho culture, sharing something so intimate puts you in a vulnerable situation. It takes a lot of courage to do what you did. Why did you decide to share this incident?

Carlos: To heal. There are many men and women who were abused like I was. I wanted to convey that you have to tell yourself that this is something that you can overcome. I don't want to be one of those people who enter a room and say, "Nice to meet you, I'm someone who was sexually abused." There are a lot of people like that, with that type of energy, who carry that burden.

Gaby: Yes, it's as if you have a label attached to you for the rest of your life . . .

Carlos: Exactly. My advice is to look in the mirror and say: "My life is not reduced to what happened to me. I am free. I am the same person that God created." I've already forgiven that man. I prayed to release him. If I had wished for him to go to hell, I would have gone with him. Instead, I thought, *I will send you to a place of light and I will forgive you.* As soon as I did, I broke free of all that anger. I didn't want to wake up every morning feeling angry and paranoid, thinking that everyone wanted to hurt me. I lived like that for a long time.

Gaby: And when did you finally forgive him?

Carlos: In the year 2007.

Gaby: Ah, very recent.

Carlos: Yes.

Gaby: And you were liberated.

Carlos: That is a beautiful word, *liberated.* If I shared all this information, it's not for people to pity me. It's to invite people to heal.

Before saying goodbye, I needed to ask him a question that had been on my mind since I saw his first music video: "Why do you make those faces when you play the guitar? What do you feel at that moment?" His answer made my jaw drop . . . and then I couldn't stop laughing! "The answer is simple, Gaby. This is like making love. If you look very pretty while you're doing it, it's because you're faking it and don't feel anything!"

A Closer Look

To watch the video with the full half-hour interview "Gaby Natale Exclusive with Carlos Santana," visit www.gabynatale.com/VirtuousCircle.

Santana talks with Gaby about:

- His devotion to the Virgin of Guadalupe.
- The keys to success.
- How he left behind his stage of excesses.

Also, enjoy the behind-the-scenes photos and discover Santana's private guitar collection.

CHAPTER 3

THE ARCHITECT: PLAN YOUR DREAM

Very near to my sunset now, I bless you, life,
because you never gave me any false hope
or unjust labor or unwarranted punishment;
because at the end of my rough road, I see
that I was the architect of my own fate,

that if I extracted honey or gall from things
it was because I instilled them with a gall or honey flavor:
when I planted rose bushes, I always harvested roses.[1]

—AMADO NERVO

#VirtuousCircle

DARE TO BE THE

Architect

OF YOUR LIFE.
IF YOU AREN'T,
OTHERS WILL BE.

@GabyNatale

Take a photo and share it online using
#VirtuousCircle

The architect is the second archetype of *the Virtuous Circle*. The task of architects is to give you their logical spirit and their obsession with creating systems and processes, helping you quantify everything so that your dreams aren't just ideas. The architect will help you design the strategies to make real everything you imagined with the help of the dreamer.

The architect is responsible, hates the unexpected, and loves planning for the future. With the architect's help, you can design an action plan that will help you realize your dreams.

You already know your architect self. It forms an important part of your personality. It's the voice within you that organizes your day-to-day life so that tomorrow you are better than today. It's the one who recommends you adjust your expenses and save money to be prepared for some unexpected event. It's the one who thinks about bringing a lunchbox with healthy food from home so as not to be tempted later. And the one who warns you that unless you focus on your studies this Sunday you won't have enough time to read everything you need for next week's final exam.

While the dreamer asks you to put your head in the clouds and unleash your imagination, the architect demands that you put your feet on the ground. The architect tells you to be strategic and use your logic to make the best possible plan of action. By the way, the word *architect* comes from the Latin *architectus*, which means the "most responsible for a project."

The architect is waiting for you with calculator and measuring tape in hand. It loves making plans, using to-do lists, and being disciplined. Under the architect's guidance you will express your dream in terms of measurable goals and objectives. Just as blue-prints come before building the house, the time to create your plan is now, before putting your dream into action!

The time has come to invoke the architect in you and create your own roadmap. Sharpen your pencil and start sketching this new chapter of your existence! Dare to be the architect of your life. If you don't do it, others will do it for you.

In This Chapter You Will Find

- An "In the First Person" section, in which I will tell you about the long road I had to travel until I accidentally discovered my dream.
- An explanation of *ikigai*, a Japanese concept that helps us define and reflect on what is our passion, profession, vocation, mission, and also our greatest dream.
- A segment called "A Voice of Authority" where an architect of life who has made history shares his path to success. He is an "architect of the sky" who began sowing fruit in the fields and ended up literally harvesting stars.
- Finally, I will share one of the most intimate decisions I've had to make to become a true architect of my personal and professional future.

In the First Person

The Wisdom of Knowing That We Don't Know

I wasn't born with a dream. For a long time, I envied those people who knew what they wanted to do since childhood, those who had such a strong desire to do something that they no longer needed to wonder what would make them happy for the rest of their lives. They knew it by heart. They could not live without doing it.

Like the future biologist fascinated by the school garden and patiently waits for the first leaf of the lettuce to appear; the boy in art class who knows that shapes, colors, and textures will accompany him forever; the teenager who knows dancing will be much more than something she does on Saturdays to have fun with friends.

In my case, it was never like that. I met my architect self after years of having a blank slate as a plan.

As a student, I didn't feel a special passion for any subject. I was not doing badly, but not tremendously well either. I was just one of the OK students who was part of the average crowd. I was never a star athlete or an honor roll student. I never won any prizes. When I graduated from high school, I went to college to study international relations. I had to work harder to continue belonging to the group of average students.

It was difficult for me to be consistent. Sometimes I managed to stay focused and take notes in class. Other times, I had my head in the clouds and not on my studies. A few times, I was really close to failing math exams because I left my algebra homework to the last minute.

Some of my classmates felt really passionate about the subjects we were learning. They went to the teachers' office hours, took extra classes to receive additional credits, and spent a large part of their summer vacation working for free to gain experience before graduating. They were true architects of their professional future.

I was not.

I didn't know if it was a lack of will, interest, or ability. I was overwhelmed by the prospect of graduating and spending the rest of my life following the protocols and conventions of the diplomatic world.

By the time I reached my junior year, I felt that something didn't make sense. We were entering the final stretch of the race, and soon we would all be graduating. Why was I not as happy as the others? I had studied for years to get to this moment! In the midst of the confusion, I had a light-bulb moment. I decided not to hide my feelings or try to convince myself that everything was fine. Rather, I had the wisdom to know . . . that I didn't know! And that was the first step to feeling better.

Although I was graduating in a few months, I signed up for a student exchange program. For four months, I would study at a London university. Maybe a change of scenery would help me figure out what was happening.

When I arrived in the English capital, I experienced a big shock. It was not a culture shock but a monetary shock! I had miscalculated how much money I needed to live in London. In the city everything was very expensive. I barely had enough money to cover rent and food.

From one day to the next, I no longer had time for soul searching. I had to start looking for work—urgently! Luckily, within a few weeks I was hired as a bartender in Piccadilly Circus.

Between my university classes and my job, I had a full schedule. It's possible that I was the worst bartender in history: since I
hardly drink alcohol, I spent most of the time getting the ingredi-
ents mixed up. Luckily, nobody really cared if I put vodka, tequila,
or gin in their cocktail. After all, the customers were drunk and
didn't notice my mistakes.

My salary was a pittance, so I had to organize my budget extremely well to stretch it as far as possible. I became an expert at
bargain hunting. But there was something I didn't want to sacrifice no matter how tight my budget: I always tried to set aside a
few pounds to go to the movies. Nothing made me happier than
watching documentaries at the end of my week!

The London Film Festival had begun. For the first time, in a
world before YouTube, I had the chance to see firsthand a selec-
tion of the best independent productions on the planet. My
burning desire to see these documentaries made me more focused than ever.

What was happening to me? I didn't recognize myself! Why did
I suddenly stop caring about buying new shoes or spending my
money on the things that had always brought me pleasure?
Where did this newly focused Gaby come from? Who was this
Gaby that didn't mind working overtime to buy tickets to watch
the next documentary? Something incredible was happening. I
had finally discovered my dream! My passion for watching those
documentaries was the key!

I didn't know how or when I was going to do it, but I promised
myself that I was going to enter the world of audiovisual production and that one day someone would be on the other side of the
screen watching the things I had created.

From that moment on, nothing was the same: now I had a direction. That dream shook me out of my confusion. It gave me a

reason to be optimistic and to get up every day wanting to start something new. Suddenly I began to experience a discipline, an enthusiasm, and a focus I had never had before. The architect started working tirelessly.

I returned to Argentina and not only finished my degree in international relations but also began studying television production at night at a media school. The following year, I graduated with a master's degree in journalism.

I am convinced that having a dream is one of the most transformative experiences we can experience.

DREAMS IMPROVE US. THEY MAKE US MORE PERSISTANT, MORE CREATIVE, MORE COURAGEOUS.

It's as if they give us superpowers. I know that when I'm feeling down, it's from my dream that I borrow my determination, my desire to create, and my strength to move forward. On behalf of my dream, I do things that I wouldn't do even for myself.

The years have gone by. It's been decades since I finished preschool. Things have changed. I no longer envy the children who would be future biologists, who were born with a dream and were fascinated by the vegetables in the school garden. Now I realize that I was not meant to be part of that group.

I was not born a dreamer. I became a dreamer over time. Because dreams, like lettuce, can also be cultivated.

THE MASTER IN THE ART OF LIVING MAKES LITTLE
DISTINCTION BETWEEN HIS WORK AND HIS PLAY, HIS
LABOR AND HIS LEISURE, HIS MIND AND HIS BODY, HIS
INFORMATION AND HIS RECREATION, HIS LOVE AND
HIS RELIGION. HE HARDLY KNOWS WHICH IS WHICH.
HE SIMPLY PURSUES HIS VISION OF EXCELLENCE AT
WHATEVER HE DOES, LEAVING OTHERS TO DECIDE
WHETHER HE IS WORKING OR PLAYING. TO HIM HE'S
ALWAYS DOING BOTH.

—JAMES A. MICHENER

BE THE ARCHITECT OF YOUR DREAM: DISCOVERING YOUR *IKIGAI* OR THAT WHICH MAKES YOU RISE EVERY MORNING

In Japan there is a region called Okinawa in which some of the most vital and long-lived people in the world are found. It's common to see centenarians there riding a bicycle, practicing martial arts, and even cultivating their own gardens. In fact, some of the lowest levels of depression in the world have been recorded in Okinawa.

But . . . what is the secret of these "young" Japanese seniors?

After decades of studies, specialists have determined that in addition to friendships, an active life, and a healthy diet, what has allowed these people to live such full lives for so many years is the development of what they call the *ikigai*. In Okinawa, the *ikigai* is a person's "reason for being." It's about your life's purpose, what makes you want to get up every morning.

Finding your *ikigai* may take time and a lot of soul searching. But the Japanese believe the effort is well worth it. They are convinced that those who discover their *ikigai* manage to live a life full of meaning and satisfaction.

Next, I will show you a graph that will help you understand the concept. It has four circles that contain:

- What you are good at (cooking, packing, etc.).
- What you love (singing, watching musicals, eating ice cream, etc.).
- What the world needs (compassion, inspiration, connection, inclusion, love, etc.).
- What you get paid for (writing, hosting shows, planning campaigns, creating content, launching platforms, etc.).

It is believed that all people are born with their own *ikigai*. That is, each of us is born to fulfill a purpose. But not everyone takes the time to discover it.

If you still don't know what yours is, would you like to discover your *ikigai*? Below, I will share the diagram I made for myself. Remember to pay special attention to where the circles intersect.

Your passion is what you are good at and what you love. In this definition of passion, we will exclude the activities for which you are paid or those that you think the world needs. In my case, for example, one could say that one of my passions is dancing. I think I'm relatively good at dancing and I love doing it, but I don't really think that the world "needs" my movements on the dance floor nor is there anyone who pays me for dancing, so this activity is perfectly classified as a passion.

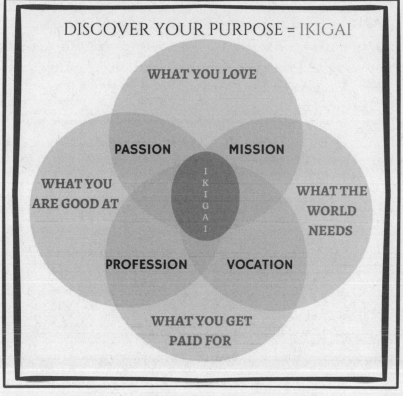

DISCOVER YOUR PURPOSE = IKIGAI

WHAT YOU LOVE

PASSION   MISSION

WHAT YOU   I K I G A I   WHAT THE
ARE GOOD AT   WORLD
                                       NEEDS

PROFESSION   VOCATION

WHAT YOU GET
PAID FOR

Ikigai.

Your profession is what you are good at and what you get paid for. This category excludes the things you love to do and that the world needs. It only refers to your talent in a paid activity. In my graphic, I included editing videos and writing scripts. These are some of the paid parts of my career that I am good at but that don't offer me much pleasure.

Your vocation is what you get paid for and what the world needs. These are not necessarily the activities you are good at or that you enjoy doing the most. Here I included creating niche content and creative project launches.

Lastly, your mission is what you love to do and what the world needs (though you don't necessarily get paid for it nor do you have to be especially good at it). Here I included volunteer work, community outreach with nonprofit organizations, solidarity events where I donated my time, and so on.

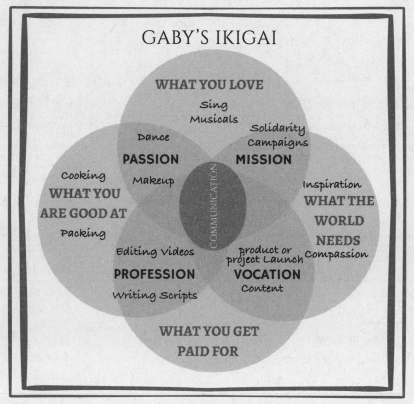

GABY'S IKIGAI

WHAT YOU LOVE
Sing
Musicals
Dance
PASSION
Solidarity
Campaigns
MISSION

Cooking
Makeup
WHAT YOU
ARE GOOD AT
Packing

COMMUNICATION

Inspiration
WHAT THE
WORLD
NEEDS

Editing Videos
PROFESSION
Writing Scripts

product or
project Launch
VOCATION
Content
Compassion

WHAT YOU GET
PAID FOR

Gaby's *Ikigai*.

In the center is the point where all the circles come together. Think about an activity that can form an invisible thread to bring them all together. That is *ikigai*. My *ikigai* is *communication*. It's what I love to do, what I am good at, what I get paid to do, and something that (humbly) I like to think the world needs or enjoys in some way.

Now it's your turn.

Take a sheet and start writing down all the activities you can think of. Don't limit yourself or your ideas. The activities you choose can be commonplace or really extraordinary. Follow your heart and don't judge your thoughts. Write down all your ideas without hesitation. Once you have the list, look at what activities correspond to each group.

Your ikigai *is in the center where what you are good at, what you love, what the world needs, and what you get paid to do meet.*

Now that you know your *ikigai*, what will make you want to get up tomorrow morning?

Something to Think About

In a small Japanese town, a woman was dying. Suddenly she had the feeling of being taken to heaven and found herself in front of her ancestors' voice.

"Who are you?" said a voice.

"I am the mayor's wife," she replied.

"I did not ask you whose wife you are, but who you are."

"I am the mother of four children."

"I didn't ask you to tell me how many children you have, but who you are."

"I am a schoolteacher."

"I didn't ask you what your profession is, but who you are."

The woman did not seem to find a satisfactory answer to the question, until she said:

"I am the one who wakes up every day to take care of my family and feed the young minds of the children in my school."

> *Thus, she passed the test and was sent back to Earth. The next morning, she woke up feeling a deep sense of meaning and purpose: she had discovered her ikigai.*
>
> —Anonymous

BE THE ARCHITECT OF YOUR PSYCHE: ARE YOU RECALCULATING OR BURSTING?

Now that you're connecting with your architect self to create your plan of action, there's one thing you should never forget: however detailed and good your plan may be, there will always be things you cannot control.

Even the most prepared architect on the planet has to deal with variables they don't control: the client may ask for last-minute changes, the approval of permits may take longer than anticipated, and there may even be an accident during construction.

Let me save you the trouble. "Perfect" plans do not exist. Your plan, like the world we live in, will never be perfect. So we better make peace with imperfection and embrace our "ferpect" plans.

Getting angry when things don't go exactly as we wanted is a guaranteed way to spend the whole day going from one fit of anger to another. There will always be problems and unexpected events! Take wedding receptions.

There are few days in our lives as carefully planned as our wedding day. On these special occasions we give our architect self free rein and we oversee planning down to the last detail. We organize in advance who will be invited to the ceremony, what the menu will be, what music will be heard during the evening, and even where each guest will be sitting. Nothing is random.

But no matter how many plans you make, life always does its magic and things don't go exactly as planned. Maybe a drunk uncle goes off script and reveals some indiscretion about the newlyweds in the middle of his speech. Or a baby has a crying fit at the precise moment when the couple are exchanging their vows. Or perhaps it's something as mundane as a rainy day, and the ceremony has to be held indoors instead of outdoors.

What will you focus on? What part of the day will stay with you? Will it be the frustration at the rain/the drunk uncle/the crying baby who tarnished our perfect plan, or will it be the loving gaze during the ring exchange?

Some say that their wedding day is the happiest day of their lives. Others think the reception is a sham because everyone has fun except the newlyweds, who spend their time running around. Who is right? Both are, probably. The answer depends on what you choose to focus on.

The key to becoming the architect of your psyche is to begin to distinguish between what you can control and what you can't.

Just as you can't control whether there will be rain on your wedding day, you can't control the traffic, unexpected difficulties, or the setbacks you face each day. What happens to you when your plan gets complicated? How do you react? Are you like the newlyweds who can't enjoy their big day because the food was cold? Or are you the type who enjoys your wedding day even if you have to dance in the rain? Remember even in circumstances out of your control, you can still be in charge of something: your reaction.

As an architect of your psyche, you always have two options when faced with a problem: recalculate or burst.

Bursting with anxiety, anger, sadness . . . bursting is often an almost automatic response when things feel like they are getting out of hand. You may burst at the traffic that doesn't move, the professor who failed you on an exam, the partner who didn't listen to you again, or the boss who denied you a promotion.

Bursting can be cathartic. After venting all your frustration, you may feel a little more relieved, but at the end of the day the matter will remain the same; the problem remains unresolved. This is the most unproductive way to react to a problem. It's voluntarily surrendering the lead role in your own life.

A life of bursting means becoming a passive actor in your life. It's giving up power and putting you at the mercy of the circumstances or people who manage to knock you off balance. Also, bursting wears you down. It saps energy. And worst of all, doing it regularly can even affect your health.

Your other option is to recalculate. Recalculating simply means using your energy to find another way.

Usually, we don't like it when the car's GPS says that annoying little word, *recalculating*. It implies that we made a wrong turn or that our journey has been complicated for some reason. No one likes it when that happens.

When things do not go as planned, however, recalculating is the best thing you can do. Recalculating gives you the power to change course and look for other options. It's your way of stepping on the accelerator and not letting anyone else decide your path. Those who recalculate take the wheel and reclaim command of their lives. With a little luck, one day the problems that almost made you burst will seem like a distant point in the rearview mirror.

You burst when:
- You blame others for your circumstances.
- You think everything depends on external factors.

- You focus your time and energy on the things you can't control.

You recalculate when:
- You know that you are responsible for your choices.
- You trust that, although there are difficulties, you have the ability to look for new paths.
- You focus your time and energy on the things you can control.

In the First Person

Recalculating as Architect of My (Future) Family

I looked at my wrists almost without recognizing them. They were full of punctures. The needles had left a trail.

I thought there would be no room left for another puncture, but I was wrong. There were still veins to prick. "I look like I came out of the movie *Trainspotting*," I said to myself. My dark humor comes out in these situations. No, I wasn't in a film about heroin addicts. Instead, I was in the same laboratory I had been to almost every day for the previous two weeks to have my blood drawn.

"In twenty-four hours, we will send the results of your blood work to Dr. Alejandro," the nurse informed me as he withdrew the syringe and put a band-aid over the prick.

As I have done my entire life when having blood drawn, I had to look away. I would say to myself: "Eyes that don't see, heart that doesn't feel (dizzy)."

I. Am. Super. Squeamish.

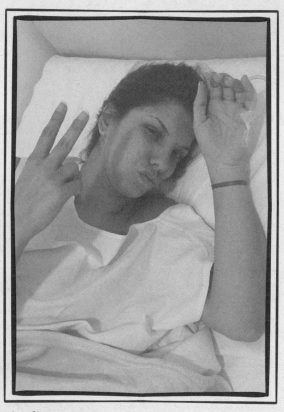

Recovering from an egg retrieval at a clinic in Buenos Aires, Argentina.

More than once while recording stories in operating rooms or morgues for television, I had to go outside and take a deep breath to avoid fainting. My world would start spinning at the sight of blood!

The next day, I had my face-to-face appointment with the gynecologist. He was waiting for me with a chart in his hand and a serious look on his face.

"Look, Gaby," he said with brutal honesty, "after age thirty-five a woman's fertility starts to drop. But it does not happen gradually; it's abrupt. If you plan on having children, you better decide soon, because you are already thirty-six."

Thank you doctor for reminding me how sexist nature is. While Mick Jagger and his peers come into the world biologically equipped to have their eighth child at seventy-two, I at thirty-something had to hurry and define what I was going to do with my life. I had to think about it, because according to what Dr. Alejandro had explained to me, my "reproductive expiration date" was just around the corner.

To put it bluntly, my clock was ticking.

My head was going a thousand miles an hour. *What if I have a baby now when I'm still young but realize later it would have been better to wait? What if I wait a little longer and then have no chance of getting pregnant? What if in a few years there are complications for having done it too late? Do I want to? Do I not want to? What do I want??? I know what I want. I want to have time to do things at my own pace. I want to have the possibility of planning my life based on my dreams and not on my biological clock.*

"I want to freeze my eggs."

This was an issue that my husband Andy and I had already discussed. Freezing my eggs, along with adoption, seemed like the best option for us. Every day I witnessed how the concept of family became more inclusive. Now, in addition to traditional families we have blended families, adoptive ones, those made up of single mothers and fathers, or same-sex couples. If the world showed me so many diverse ways of forming a family, why not open my mind to an expanded idea of motherhood?

All my life I sought freedom: creative freedom. Economic freedom. The freedom to choose who to love or with whom to spend my time. If I loved freedom so much, why not also seek my own reproductive freedom?

That was how I became an architect of my own family plan and started the treatment.

The *vitrification of oocytes* (the scientific name of the procedure) is a relatively new technique that allows us to extend a woman's fertility by collecting and storing eggs for later use. The first baby conceived through a preserved egg was born in 1986. Since then, thousands of children around the world have been born every year through this process.

Not everything in the garden is rosy, however. The treatment also has its disadvantages. It can be painful and—as in any medical procedure—there is no guarantee of success. To top it all off, it's not cheap (each cycle costs around $15,000 in the United States, 5,000 euros in Spain, and between $3,000 and $6,000 in Latin America).

The conversations Andy and I had in preparation for the procedure made us feel like we were part of a movie. We went from jokes about the possible side effects of so many hormones (*"Doctor, have mercy, how serious can my wife's mood swings be?"*) to serious and even macabre talks after filling out the clinic's legal forms (*If the patient dies during the procedure, but the eggs are successfully frozen, who will be designated as the owner of the genetic material? Will the deceased's frozen eggs be discarded or preserved?*).

For me, the treatment entailed an additional difficulty: though I hate needles, I would have to learn to give myself hormone injections. A *lot* of injections.

For weeks, I would inject varying doses the doctor would establish based on my blood levels. Just thinking about the needles made my head spin.

My husband, who knows how squeamish I am, offered to administer the injections. I politely refused his help. In all honesty . . . he seemed more scared than me!

After the initial shock, I decided to just take things slowly. Perhaps part of what I needed to learn from this was to face my fears.

The doctor had given us some videos with step-by-step instructions on how to prepare the syringe and drugs. The night of my first injection I looked at the needles again and again. I watched the tutorial and prepared the syringe. I filled it and wiped my abdomen with an alcohol pad. Without hesitation, I grabbed my skin, pulled it into a small protruding roll, pushed the needle in, and emptied the syringe. *Bam!* As I removed the needle, I was relieved that I had done what I was so afraid of doing. Making peace with the needles had been much easier than I thought!

I learned to fill the syringe and administer the drugs, to read the tick marks on the barrel, and even to tap the syringe to remove any air bubbles trapped inside. In total, I had to give myself twenty-five injections.

Some days seemed like something out of a comedy. The drugs had to be kept refrigerated and be administered at specific times. So if we wanted to go to dinner with friends, we could go only to restaurants two blocks or less from our where we were staying.

Once, having dinner at a cantina, injection time arrived. I discreetly excused myself for a few minutes and asked the waiter to please keep my food warm.

Never in a million years could the people in the restaurant have guessed that between the appetizer and the main course I sneaked out to inject myself!

The day before the egg retrieval, when I took the last hormone injection, I was so proud that I filmed myself explaining the process. I had become an expert on needles!

The next day, I went into the operating room satisfied that I had done my part. When I woke up from the anesthesia, the first thing I saw was my husband's smiling face. He was amusing himself by taking a commemorative close up of my sleepy self (which appears at the beginning of this section) and announcing that everything had gone well.

For me, thinking about motherhood in a broad and unconventional way means freeing myself from the tyranny of a life racing against the clock. Vitrification and adoption are my declarations of independence. They give me the possibility to plan my family on my own terms.

Sometimes, making decisions is not easy, but I don't want to let fears stop me.

I prefer to freeze them!

SOME PRACTICAL SUGGESTIONS TO FEED THE ARCHITECT IN YOU

- *Distinguish between what you can control and what you cannot control.* The most efficient plans are the ones made knowing that there are unknowable variables. Anticipating scenarios and creating alternative plans makes difficult situations in which you have little or no control much more manageable.

- *Small steps add up to achieve big goals.* Divide big goals into smaller goals. Now divide those smaller goals into lists of achievable tasks. Make a plan to perform these tasks every day or on a regular basis. Simple tasks performed consistently produce great results. Imagine adding them up for a year. It's better to do something (whether it's a little or a lot) every day than to wait and try to do everything at the last moment, racing against the clock.

  For example, if you never went to college and you think the only way to graduate is to quit the job you depend on to live and spend four years studying full-time, it's going to be pretty hard for you to decide to take those college courses.

But what would happen if you changed the focus? Perhaps that four-year program has an intermediate degree that takes just one or two years to complete. You can start by studying part time while continuing to work. Once you have that intermediate degree, your work options will certainly improve. This will give you extra motivation to continue studying and finish the full program. With time and at your own pace, you can earn your degree and achieve what seemed at first impossible.

- *Be an architect of your energy.* Learning to be conscious stewards of our energy is one of the most difficult tasks. Not everything or everyone is equally important. Every day you will come across situations or people that can disrupt your peace. As difficult as it may seem, try to not allow them to. Your inner peace depends exclusively on you. People can't disrupt your peace unless you let them.

Seeking, maintaining, and protecting your emotional well-being is part of the job when you are the architect of your psyche. Sometimes it's difficult not to feel affected when you are the target of unfair comments or unpleasant situations. But at the end of the day the most important thing is to decide which situation or comment really deserves your attention. Is that person or problem that's about to disrupt your peace really a concrete threat to your dream or your happiness? If not, just move on. Don't wear yourself out with something that isn't worthwhile. You will need your time and energy to devote to what is valuable. At the end of the day, the really important things in life are few.

BE THE ARCHITECT OF YOUR PLAN:
WATCH OUT FOR THE LIE OF BINARY DREAMS

The world of computing is governed by a language called *binary code*. It is a numbering system with only two digits: zero and one. A quality is attributed to each number. Zero means off, one means on. Basically, it's the same logic a light switch uses.

For many, dreams also seem to be written in binary. If a dream does not come true or "turn on" in a certain amount of time, they discard it and remain in "off mode" forever. This is the same logic used by those who abandon their diet the first time they can't resist a slice of cake. It's as if that great shame is so unacceptable it's better to throw the entire diet overboard!

This binary vision of dreams is the main reason why most people give up. "This is what I always wanted, what I tried to achieve, and it didn't work," many say to themselves. So, without further ado, the dream ends up in the trash can.

That is why the binary model is poisonous for dreamers.

If you conceive your goals, projects, or dreams as a challenge in the style of "all or nothing," you will be paralyzed. Any setback will serve as an excuse to tell yourself that your dream is impossible. Thus, many attainable dreams and objectives are discarded prematurely.

What would happen to the drop of water that drips on the stone if it used the binary model to measure its potential? After dripping on the stone a couple of times, it would probably abandon its task and give up, without knowing that its nature and destiny entail the possibility of breaking through the stone.

If you are one of those people who live your life using the binary model, examine yourself with sincerity. What would happen to your dreams if you gave them permission to have more modes than just on and off?

Let us now consider our aspirations in a different way. There is another model that also comes from technology and is much more appropriate when thinking about our dreams. It is called the *incremental innovation* model.

Incremental innovation raises the possibility of reaching a desired result from a growing and staggered process. It's the kind of gradual innovation that can be seen in the evolution of the wheel: the rudimentary stone wheels of prehistory gave way to elaborate wagon wheels and eventually to the sophisticated rubber wheels we use in modern cars.

If you apply this model when you think of your dreams, you will be able to go far beyond on and off. No longer are the only options to get it right or to get it wrong.

Your dreams will be the result of a succession of continuous and cumulative advances.

By following this model, you will become aware that each step forward is not only valuable but also a precondition for the next. If you begin to see your dreams from this new perspective, what reason could you have to give them up?

The irony is that by replacing the binary model with incremental innovation, you end up achieving just what you were looking for in the beginning: having your dream always "on."

•   •   •

A Voice of Authority

Astronaut José Hernández

AN "INCREMENTAL" DREAM THAT WENT FROM EARTH TO SPACE

One of the stories about an "incremental" dream that has affected me most is that of astronaut José Hernández. When I had the privilege of meeting him, I was fascinated by this Mexican immigrant's tenacity.

Pictured with astronaut José Hernández. From his childhood in the agricultural fields to his rise to space on the shuttle *Discovery*, José is model of perseverance.

José was born in a humble family of farmers. He spent his childhood constantly moving between Michoacán, Mexico, and California to help his family harvest fruits and vegetables. Although he was just a child, his workdays were hard, beginning at four in the morning and ending when the sun went down.

Throughout his childhood, school was a problem for José. The moving around with his family didn't allow him to be consistent with his studies. The pace of work forced him to go from school to school. As a result, he missed three months of classes every year.

When he reached high school, he lagged behind his peers. It wasn't until the beginning of his adolescence that he managed to learn to speak English fluently and to understand what he was being taught in class.

Despite the simplicity of his life, José looked at the sky and had big dreams. When he was just a nine-year-old boy, in the middle of a family dinner, he watched the television fascinated by the first images of humankind landing on the moon. Little José was so struck that he made a decision right then and there that would leave a mark on his destiny: in the middle of dinner, he announced to his family that he had decided to become an astronaut.

Instead of laughing and taking it as a silly childhood dream, Mr. Hernández became serious: "Son, if you really want to do it and you work hard, you're going to do it."

The years passed and the Hernández family managed to stop moving and settled in Stockton, California. Studying in the same school throughout the year allowed little José to focus on his studies and recover lost time.

His father's words had been etched in his mind, and he concentrated on taking every science and mathematics class he could. It was not easy, but he immersed himself in books with the same effort he had put into working in the fields. Within a few years, he was able to finish high school as an honor student.

Focused on taking the next step in his dream, José kept looking at the stars. He knew that the only way to accomplish his dream was to study engineering. Five years later, José became an engineer. He was beside himself with joy. After so much time, he was one step away from fulfilling his dream of being an astronaut! It was a dream he had been fighting for since he was nine.

But things don't always turn out as planned. José still had a long road ahead of him to make his dream come true—a road almost as long and complex as the one between the stars and the fields in which he had spent his childhood.

The problem was that, despite being an engineer and doing his best, NASA's strict training program didn't accept José as part of its team. As much as he tried and tried, he always got the same answer: a resounding no.

This dreamer still had a long way to go. Rather, eleven long ways to go, because NASA rejected José's request eleven times. On his twelfth attempt, this immigrant from Michoacán achieved his dream of becoming an astronaut.

José says that the key to avoid being discouraged and to continue persevering was to stay focused. Every time a door was closed, he asked what he should do to improve next time. Instead of being offended, with each rejection he was learning what he needed to do to move forward. He knew that every refusal brought him closer to his goal.

Finally, in 2009, José joined NASA as an astronaut. From space, he looked down at Earth, the planet whose soil he had cultivated for so many years with his own bare hands and found that not even the stars are out of reach for those who dream with their whole being.

José's Advice to Be the Architect of Your Own Plan:

"First, decide what you want to be in life, what your goal is. After that, recognize how far you are from achieving it. Then, create a plan or route to achieve your goal. Next, get ready, study. Finally, dedicate the same amount of effort as those who work in the fields every day. If you mix all that together, you have the recipe to succeed in life."

THE ARCHITECT— OPTIONAL EXERCISE: THINKING AND PLANNING YOUR DREAM IN DETAIL

I prepared this exercise for those who still do not know how to define their dream or for those who want to go deeper into the planning and conceptualization of it. It is an optional exercise. If you feel that you are ready to move on, you can go straight to the next chapter of *The Virtuous Circle*. On the other hand, if you think it would be good to get to know your architect self more deeply, this exercise is perfect for you.

I want you to spend a minute imagining the house of your dreams. Stop to think about every detail of that home:

- Where would it be located? In your hometown or somewhere far away?
- What kind of landscape? A tropical beach, a pine forest, or perhaps you are one of those people who love to live in a sophisticated skyscraper overlooking a big city?
- How big would it be? Do you prefer a small and cozy house or a large and imposing mansion?

Now that you have the *mental image* of what the house would be like, your next step is to meet with a professional architect, the one who helps you move from imagination to action.

The more clarity and detail your mental image of the house has, the easier it will be to "translate" that idea into something real. To move forward, you will probably have to ask yourself some questions.

The first group of questions will focus on defining and understanding what the house you imagined is like. Those are the questions intended to understand the *concept* of the house.

Examples of Concept Questions

What are the specific characteristics of the house? What makes it different from any other? Why is this house suitable for you?

When the concept of the house has been defined, it will be time to answer a second group of questions. These questions will have to do with the *practical aspects of building* your home. These are questions about the realization of the house.

Examples of Realization Questions

- Priorities: *What are the foundations upon which this house will remain standing? Which parts of it are fundamental and which are secondary?*
- Elements: *What resources are required to build this house? What professional skills or techniques are necessary to build it?*
- Project stages: *What processes are needed to build this house? In what order should these be followed?*
- Timelines: *How much time do you anticipate you will need to build the house?*

One reason why a professional architect will ask you so many questions is to be a "bridge" between the image in your head and the house that will be built brick by brick in the real world.

In this exercise, the roles are very clear: you are the one who imagines the ideal house and the professional architect is the one who helps you find the best way to transform that idea into reality.

But what would happen if instead of building a house you are building your dream?

That's a task that no one else can do for you. You are the one who has to do the work of the architect!

Your task will be to have the clearest possible mental image of the dream (concept) and define the best plan to bring it to reality (realization). For that, you must be ready to answer the same type of questions that you answered about the house, only this time you will do it with your dream in mind.

Are you ready?

Below is an exact copy of the questions you read above. The only change is that the word *house* has been replaced by the word *dream*. It's time to summon the architect in you to begin defining the concept and realization of your dream.

Examples of Concept Questions
What are the specific characteristics of your dream? What sets it apart from any other? Why is this dream right for you?

Examples of Execution Questions
- Priorities: *What are the foundations upon which this dream will remain standing? Which parts of it are really fundamental and which are secondary?*
- Elements: *What resources are required to build this dream? What professional skills or techniques are necessary to build it?*
- Project stages: *What processes are needed to build this dream? In what order should these be followed?*
- Timelines: *How much time do you anticipate you will need to build the dream?*

Answer the architect's questions with complete sincerity. Write them down on a piece of paper. You will see that you have the basic elements of your dream and you know how to take the first steps to carry it out. At the end of the exercise, you should have a few ideas to complete the following sentences:

Starting to Define the CONCEPT of Your Dream
- My dream is . . .

- The specific characteristics of my dream are . . .
- My dream makes me happy and is good for me because . . .
  (it allows me to express myself, it gives me creative
  freedom, it opens a new stream of income, it is my true
  vocation, it will help me improve my health, it will allow
  me to connect with interesting people, etc.).

Starting to define the EXECUTION of your dream

- Priorities: To achieve my dream, the three most
  important goals that will make me move forward are . . .
- New skills: To conquer my dream I need to learn to . . .
- Strengths: Of the personal skills I already have, my
  strengths in support of this dream are . . . (I am optimistic,
  organized, I already know some of the things I need,
  etc.).
- Areas to improve: The most important skills I need to
  improve to achieve my dream are . . . (I need to learn
  more about coding, become a confident public speaker,
  get certified in a specialty, learn more about my dream,
  etc.).
- Basic resources: The *minimum* I need to start developing
  my dream is . . . (The key here is the word *minimum*.
  Think about the first thing you need to get moving).
- Resources in my favor: Some things I already have that I
  need for my dream are . . . (List everything that comes to
  mind. Do not look at the glass as half empty. You may
  already have many useful things that you take for granted
  such as Internet access, email, a computer, etc.).
- Resources to get: The first resources or things I need to
  start putting my dream into action are . . .

- My support network: The people or organizations that could help me to fulfill my dream are . . . (Here you can include specialists, friends, family, colleagues, mentors, educational institutions, professionals, financial organizations, etc.).
- Timelines: I intend to meet my first three objectives by . . .

CHAPTER 4

THE MAKER: EXECUTE YOUR DREAM

A path, if you don't walk it, you never arrive.
A piece of land, if you don't cultivate it, never bears fruit.
A business, if you don't attend it, never thrives.
A man, if not educated, never improves.

A job, if you don't start it, you never finish it.
A book, if you don't apply it, you never understand.

—ASIAN PROVERB

#VIRTUOUSCIRCLE

IT'S ONLY
Impossible
IF YOU DON'T TRY.

@GABYNATALE

Take a photo and share it online using
#VirtuousCircle

The maker is the third archetype of *the Virtuous Circle*. The maker arrives in your life to set your desire in motion. Your maker self teaches you that the perfect moment doesn't exist, that you are much freer than you think, and sometimes it's best to think less and do more. The maker knows you are ready to embark on the adventure even if you're still not feeling up to it!

In your maker self you will find an accomplice who will give you the final push you need to get rid of doubts and start moving forward. Under the maker's pragmatic guidance you will begin to execute the ideas you conceived with the dreamer and the plans you devised with the architect. With the maker's help you can create, invent, or execute what you need so that your personal transformation goes from theory to practice.

Your maker self reaffirms what you already know: *that staying in the same place to avoid facing your fears will not give you the security you are looking for.* In fact, it will have the opposite effect. In a world undergoing constant change, there is nothing riskier than stagnation and clinging to what you already know.

The maker is a familiar ally. It has lived in you for a long time. The maker is that inexplicable impulse that leads you to dare, to go for more, and to keep moving forward even when you are scared.

The maker was by your side when you were just a child and you had the courage to ride a bike without training wheels for the first time. The maker patted your back when you overcame fear and declared your love to that special person. It gave you the courage to speak in public on the first day of school in front of a room full of new classmates. The maker was the extra dose of audacity that you demonstrated by standing up to your boss and receiving a long overdue promotion.

The maker believes in you and demands that you too believe in yourself. It reminds you that the only thing impossible is the thing you don't try. That you cannot be a "maker of greatness" out in the world unless you first embrace the greatness that lives inside of you. That to achieve what you have never achieved you must dare to do what you have never done.

The ones who make are brave: they face their fears and the scrutiny of prying eyes.

The ones who make arrive at the truth: only those who cheer themselves discover the limits of possibility.

The ones who make are consistent: they teach not through words but through their actions.

The ones who make are immortal: they defy their earthly limits with a legacy that lives on forever.

Human beings find a higher plane in the creative and maker capacity. It's no accident that sacred texts of different religions refer to their god as the "Supreme Maker."

In ancient Greece, it was believed that the great actions of men were the result of a heavenly intervention. If they gave good speeches, created majestic buildings, or were excellent mathematicians, the real "makers" behind their talents were the gods of Olympus, who expressed their power through human labor. For the Greeks, being a "maker" consisted of igniting an inner spark that connected them to the divine and allowed them access to an inexhaustible well of ideas.

On the other hand, for Indian leader Mahatma Gandhi, to make was not necessarily a divine act but a prerequisite for people to aspire to fulfillment. He was convinced that the happiness people want can be attained only when what one thinks, what one says, and what one does are in harmony.

The maker arrives bringing with it a great gift: the possibility that actions, words, and ideas can be aligned with one another. It's the unique opportunity to travel life in congruence and not in contradiction with your desires.

We all come into the world equipped with extraordinary tools. Our job is to bring those hidden treasures into the light.

The Maker versus the Apprentice

Before continuing, I would like to make a clarification. The maker and the apprentice (the archetype of the next chapter) are intimately related, since both guide and accompany us at the moment when we begin to put our vision into practice. They force us to question ourselves and ask what happens to us as the plans we make with the architect go from the imaginary to reality.

For clarity's sake, I will cover different issues in each of these two chapters.

- In "The Maker" I will consider how starting down the path of personal transformation can modify the dynamics of our relationships with the people around us and how it can bring into focus our own priorities.
- In "The Apprentice," on the other hand, I will focus on the aspects related to the development of the mental framework that most favors learning and the perfection of our abilities.

• • •

In This Chapter You Will Find

- "The Maker's Thermometer," an easy method to think about your own way of doing and discovering your *optimal sustainable performance range.*
- "A Voice of Authority," where Gaby sits down with Chilean American writer Isabel Allende to discuss the ups and downs on her journey toward becoming the most read Latina writer in the world with more than seventy million books sold.
- "Tips to Take Care of Your Maker Self," where we will analyze the relationship between your and other people's passage through the Virtuous Circle. We will see how to anticipate others' responses when you start down the path of personal transformation, and we will learn how to identify allies and negative people in your own environment.
- Two "In the First Person" sections are included: "Lola Superstar—Bad People or Bad Moments?" and "We Are All Connected—The Story of Nelva, My Grandmother and Ally."

THE MAKER THERMOMETER: DISCOVERING YOUR OPTIMAL SUSTAINABLE PERFORMANCE

Every time I get on a plane, I watch them with envy. They are the travelers in sandals and shorts. You can see them in every airport in the world regardless of the time of the year. I have christened them

"Aloha Travelers," because they look like they just came from some Hawaiian resort.

The "Aloha Travelers" look unconcerned, as if they had taken advantage of every minute possible at the beach and then without much thought grabbed their suitcases and went to the airport without changing. How nice it would be to be an "Aloha Traveler" for a day!

My air travel preparations are the opposite of these travelers in sandals. I have to plan everything, because I'm always freezing cold wherever I go. Call me an "Eskimo Traveler" if you want. I won't be offended.

My wardrobe and carry-on luggage are never left to chance. Since I'm always colder than most other people, I worry about taking all the proper sweaters and coats. If I don't take precautions, hours of freezing cold await me once the airplane doors close. That's why I have developed several travel preparation techniques. In general, these include dressing in layers of warm clothes (almost always black so the wrinkles don't show as much) and carrying my own travel blankets, or an elegant wool poncho if I want to look extra fancy.

For "Aloha Travelers," traveling as I do would be a nightmare; they would spend the entire flight sweating and dehydrated. For me, flying like them (in sandals and shorts) would be insufferable torture, ensuring that I reach my destination sneezing and a step or two away from catching a cold.

The same goes for how you see effort: each person sees it differently. What for one may require maximum exertion may not even challenge another. That's why it's worth exploring *your own ideal combination* of focus and relaxation. One way to do it is through what I call the "Maker's Thermometer."

The "Maker's Thermometer" is a scale. On the left, there's total relaxation. On the right, there's maximum focus and effort.

The further to the left you move, the more your activities will include immediate gratification and leisure: a greater number of vacations, impulse buys, shorter working hours, and other things that give you instant satisfaction.

The further to the right you move, the closer you will be to the activities that require focus, commitment, and delayed gratification. These activities include saving for the future, extended working hours, healthy living habits, and other things like that.

When it comes to deploying the power of your maker self, it's essential that you begin to define your *optimal sustainable performance range*. Somewhere along this scale lies a section just right for

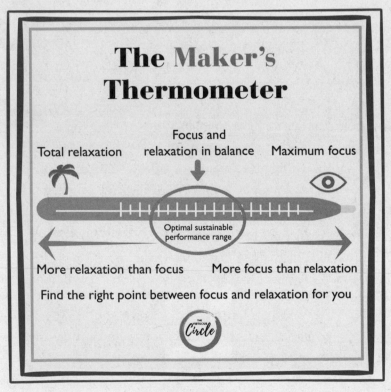

The Maker's Thermometer.

you to be and work your best. This range represents the appropriate balance between focus and relaxation for you. It may involve working a certain number of hours, going on vacation, taking time off a certain number of times a year, or having a specific ratio of savings to expenses.

If you go too far to the left toward relaxation, your performance will not be optimal. There will be too many distractions. Your experience may be pleasant and full of immediate satisfaction, but with such a low level of commitment your future results will be very uncertain.

If you go too far to the right toward focus, your performance will not be sustainable. Your path will offer you so little enjoyment that you will want to give up after a while, because no one can work without breaks or rewards. In addition, you're likely to damage your health or relationships irreparably over time.

The only way to find your ideal combination is by trying out different options.

Some will prefer to have more time today, even though that means less chance of having knowledge or money tomorrow, or perhaps it's is the other way around. You may discover things that you are unwilling to sacrifice for anything in the world. But the opposite may also be possible. You may be surprised to find that you are willing to make more concessions than you originally thought in order to fight for your dream.

Best of all is that, unlike the temperature on the plane, the optimal sustainable performance lies in a range of values, not just at one point.

Make a list of the activities that are a priority as you work toward your dreams, those that give you pleasure and those that you have to do every day. Now look at the thermometer and place them where they belong on the scale between total relaxation and maximum focus.

You can try different combinations to test your range's upper and lower limits. Then you will discover if you prefer to add more focus or if you can achieve the same results by adding more relaxation.

Here is a diagram of the "Maker's Thermometer" that I made for myself based on this moment in my life when I am writing this book and working on several new projects.

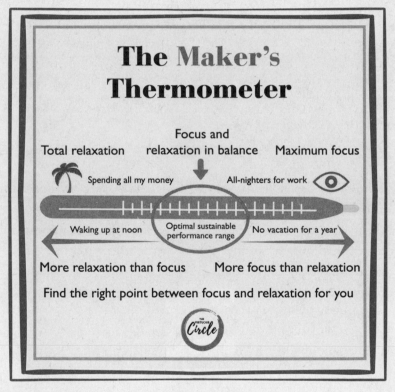

Gaby's Thermometer.

In the middle is my own range of *optimal sustainable performance*. On the right, there are two examples of things I am not willing to do: (1) spend a whole year without taking at least a few days of vacation and (2) pulling all-nighters.

There have been times in my life when things have been intense, so I've had to be flexible regarding these two. But I've learned that I can't spend years without taking time off or regularly pulling all-nighters. I can do these things under exceptional circumstances, but they are not *sustainable* over time.

No important long-term project is ruined by a vacation, nor is it "saved," if it is really in trouble, by pulling an all-nighter. So I choose to leave all-nighters and no vacations outside my *range of optimal sustainable performance*.

On the other hand, I know that I need order and structure to do my best. That's why on the left side of my circle there are two other things that, based on my criteria, are activities that are too relaxed: (1) sleeping until noon and (2) spending my whole paycheck. If I embraced those options, I would be undermining my ability to perform *optimally*.

The good thing about the Maker's Thermometer is that you can adjust the *optimal sustainable performance range* according to where you are in your life or which project you are working on. As you may know, in the beginning you will have to position yourself further to the right of the scale to have the greatest possible focus, but once you achieve your first goals you can adjust it further to the left if you need to.

The Maker's Thermometer is an exercise worth doing. You will discover what your priorities really are, how to optimize your performance, and the keys to making it sustainable in the long term.

Some Questions to Think About in Your Own Maker's Thermometer

- What are the sacrifices YOU WOULD be willing to make for your dream? (E.g., work at different times or days, use your weekends to study or work, live far away from your loved ones, etc.).

- What are the sacrifices you WOULD NOT be willing to make for your dream? (E.g., move, stop spending special dates with your loved ones, etc.).
- What is the range of hours per day or week you would be willing to devote to your dream?
- What is the minimum and maximum vacation time or relaxation time you feel comfortable with?
- What are the changes that YOU WOULD and WOULD NOT be willing to make in your finances on the way to your dream? (E.g., save a larger percentage of your income, pay debts, reinvest your money in training to learn new skills, use the money you spend on having fun now to instead buy the things you need for your dream).

In the First Person

Lola Superstar—
Bad People or Bad Moments?

Not all the people we meet on our journey are good or bad. There are gray areas.

This is a true story I decided to include to reflect on the importance of not rushing to judge others but rather stopping for a minute and differentiating between bad people . . . and bad moments.

As soon as I entered the office, my production team gave me a message: while I was in the bathroom, I had received a call from Lola Superstar, the legendary presenter of Spanish television.

"She left you a message," they informed me. "It says she sent us an email by mistake and that she's extremely sorry and embarrassed. Please, don't read it, don't give it any importance, and delete it immediately."

Our editor, Jeremiah, was dying of curiosity. He couldn't stand the suspense. He risked asking mischievously: "Could it be that she accidentally sent us intimate photos?" To tell you the truth, he sounded a little excited. Lola Superstar was a stunning beauty. I'm sure he would have loved to catch a glimpse of those private photos, if they existed, at least out of the corner of his eye!

I checked my personal email, but there was nothing from her in my inbox. Maybe it was a mistake.

We were in a rush to wrap up the next week's show, I asked them to ignore the mysterious call from Lola Superstar. I would look into it later. Right now, the most important thing was to meet our deadline and make sure everything was ready for the next *SuperLatina* broadcast.

That day had been especially good. We had just issued a press release announcing that the largest cosmetics brand on the planet (a famous French brand) had chosen me as its ambassador and correspondent on the red carpet of the Latin Grammys. *SuperLatina* and its team would be in Las Vegas doing all the coverage for them. It was an amazing opportunity!

Later, a producer forwarded an email that had arrived in the inbox we use for press releases. It was Lola's.

Now I understood why she had called in upset, asking us to erase her message! Lola had written an email to her manager about our press release. But in her haste, she had made a

mistake. Instead of *forwarding* the release to the intended recip-
ient, she had pressed *reply* and sent her message to us.

She had unintentionally sent us the following email:

Dear [name of Lola Superstar's manager]:

*Opportunities like this one from Gaby Natale's announce-
ment are what we should be working on and looking for. She
is doing great!*

*It would be good to get together and study what she's
doing, see who she's partnering with, and contact them or
their competitors.*

*Between you and me. I have a lot more experience than
Gaby, a better sense of fashion and, although it sounds bad,
I'm prettier (I'm Lola Superstar after all. Ha!).*

Tell me what you think.

L.

Ouch! My first reaction was surprise. The only thing she didn't
criticize was my dog (or rather my cat, Bombona)!

I had spent time with Lola Superstar on different occasions,
and although we weren't friends, she had not seemed particularly
hostile or competitive. On the contrary, I liked her a lot!

The second thing I noticed was my lack of anger. Any other
time, I would have been furious. Lola Superstar had cataloged me
as kind of ugly, a novice, and with little sense of fashion. She even
planned to try to steal my sponsors! Why wasn't I angry and calling to insult her?

It was hard for me to think that Lola was a monster. I felt that
it was not her but her insecurity that was reflected in the email. I
realized that hidden among the insults, the unfriendly mail expressed a feeling not completely foreign to me: frustration. Lola

was looking for opportunities and felt that others (in this case me) were "stealing" them.

That's when I finally understood why I hadn't gotten angry: *I had been like Lola once.*

I had also had moments when I felt that opportunities were slipping away. I had also had moments when I had criticized others. I had also had moments where I gave in to the temptation and thought that others' triumphs meant one less opportunity for me. No. Lola Superstar was not a bad person. She was just having a bad moment.

I kept thinking about it and recognized an awkward truth: I also had my own "Lola Superstar moment" and owed someone an apology. It occurred several years before, but I still remembered it. The time had come to make peace with the past.

In my first job in front of the cameras in the United States, I felt tremendously insecure. I had been hired as the main news anchor on the leading television channel in the Midland-Odessa market in West Texas. I would be in charge of the news, and I was happy to have the opportunity! I was particularly excited to host the weekend community show. It had a much more versatile format than the news. It was perfect for me!

But not everything was perfect. Like any novice, I was full of fears.

I knew that my job was extremely competitive. My boss, the news director, didn't miss an opportunity to remind me that he constantly received resumes from candidates interested in my job.

For me, the pressure was threefold—professional, legal, and familial. I was not a citizen or a resident of the United States at the time, I had only a temporary work permit, and to top it off my salary (which was no fortune) was our only household income.

I felt like prey in a precarious situation with a lot at stake. If I lost my job, I would not only be unemployed, but my husband,

Andy, and I would also be left without legal status and would have to leave the United States to start over who knows where.

One day, my boss called me to a special meeting. He wanted to tell me that I would soon have a new coworker: Perla C., a very popular radio host from the city who would join the team. Before the meeting was over, with his usual casual tone, he dropped a bomb on me: "I almost forgot; I changed my mind. It will no longer be you but Perla C. hosting the weekend community show."

I lowered my head and swallowed my pride. I had been excited about that show for months, but I knew I had too much to lose if I complained! Even though I was humiliated, I told him that everything was fine and returned to my desk.

On the outside I kept up appearances, but on the inside, I was furious! *Who did Perla C. think she was to come and steal* MY *opportunities? Why were they giving her* MY *weekend show?* From that moment on, I had Perla C. in my sights.

When she arrived on her first day of work, I received her with a barely civil greeting. I had given a warm welcome and a tour of the station to other coworkers in the newsroom, but I hardly spoke to the "show thief."

My insecurity began to skyrocket! I kept an eye on what Perla C. did, and of course I automatically disliked all her comments. Anything she proposed in the meetings seemed awful to me. I did my best to interact with her as little as possible and only when necessary. Everything she did raised my suspicions. If she had taken one of my shows, what would stop her from taking over my position?

To make matters worse, my boss loved Perla C., and he spent all day telling me how wonderful she was. He would say that Perlita had said this or Perlita had said that, that Perlita had done one thing or another thing . . . I was sick and tired of hearing about Perlita! But like any good masochist, I tormented myself by watching her show every Sunday. I was suffering like crazy. It had been months since the premiere, but I was still very angry to see that "usurper" occupying the chair that had been promised to me.

One day, we ended up in the same editing booth. I was annoyed that I was forced to share a few minutes with the "show thief" while waiting for a video file to be copied.

It was the first time we had to spend a few minutes alone. As usual, I kept to myself. I wasn't interested in having any deep or long conversations with her. Instead, I filled the awkward moments with chit chat. I told her that I had just gotten a French manicure and that I loved how it looked on camera. As soon as my video was copied, I said goodbye to Perla C. and quickly left, relieved to end the exchange between us.

When I arrived at work the next day, there was a small package on my desk. It was a French manicure kit. Perla C. had left me a surprise gift. I felt like a fool. Such a generous gesture was the last thing I expected from my "arch nemesis."

Perla C. had taught me a great lesson. Since she had come to work with us, I had behaved like a petulant girl. I held her responsible for my bosses' decisions and gave her the cold shoulder as if every opportunity I missed at the station was somehow her fault. I had been tremendously unfair. Now, "the usurper" brought me a little gift.

Despite my hostility, my sharp answers, and my suspicious glances, Perla C. had had the wisdom to not return insecurity with insecurity. She had been able to rise above an "eye for an eye" and had given me an olive branch . . . in the shape of a French manicure kit!

For some reason, when I received Lola Superstar's unfriendly email, the manicure kit that Perla C. gave me came to mind. I also had to give Lola a second chance! But before writing a reply to

Lola, I wanted to do what I should have done long ago: apologize to Perla C.

So I sent her the Facebook message you see reproduced below:

> Hello Perla,
> I hope you are having a beautiful Sunday. I've been want-ing to write to you for quite some time. I wanted to tell you something that I have been dealing with for several years. I think that when you came to the television station, I was a very cold and territorial coworker. The truth is that I felt tremendously insecure and at risk, because my work visa depended on me being able to keep that job. In addition, my husband's immigration status also depended on mine, so I felt quite a lot of pressure. I want to apologize if that coldness ever bothered you or made you suffer. You taught me a great lesson even though you were "the new girl" at work. You did it by facing my coldness with a smile, kind gestures, and even a little gift (a manicure kit, do you re-member?). I felt like a fool for being so insecure around someone whom I could tell was a good person. It's been a long time, but it's better late than never to apologize for the things we're not proud of, right? I'm sending you a big hug! Gaby

And she replied like this:

> What exists in my mind and heart, with respect to you, is great admiration and respect for how hard you work to ac-complish your life projects and to be better every day. I will keep holding on to that great human being in you, with the humility you have had in offering an apology, which makes

me admire you even more. And you know something? Every-
thing that happened when we worked together at Univision
was left behind; I don't even remember it. It's as if it never
happened to me! Here is a big hug and a thousand bless-
ings to you and yours!

It was very comforting to receive such a beautiful response
from Perla C.!

She taught me that sometimes it is worth pausing to see people beyond any particular attitude they display in the moment
Good people also have bad moments. *Who would have imag-*
ined that there would be such a wise life lesson in a simple man-
icure kit?

I sat in front of the computer and wrote a friendly email to
Lola. How could I not understand her if only a few years prior I
had been like Lola Superstar to Perla C.?

The big difference between Lola and me was that in my moments of weakness with Perla C. I could let off steam in private.
Lola, on the other hand, had had the bad luck that a mistake left
her exposed and her words found their way to me. How could I
get angry?

I chose to tell this story because I feel that sometimes pride
plays a trick on us and we rush into rivalries. Now, every time I
encounter a bitter episode, I stop for a minute to ask myself: *Is it*
a bad person or a bad moment?

As I had anticipated, Lola was no monster. She answered my
email telling me that she felt tremendously sorry for what had
happened and that she had no intention of hurting me.

We gave each other a second chance and turned the page. I
hope that if she ever reads this book and recognizes herself, she
will be pleased to learn about the "domino effect" this little incident between us generated.

And if, on the contrary, she doesn't like finding her story here, just in case . . . I will wait a few days before checking my email again!

Story of a Samurai: The Gift of Insults

An ancient Japanese tale tells us about an elderly samurai living on the outskirts of a big city. Everyone admired him, and it was known that in his younger years he had fought honorably in countless battles.

Now that the passage of time no longer allowed him to fight, the old samurai was dedicated to instructing the youth. Each afternoon he met with his apprentices and taught them, sharing with them the wisdom he had learned after so many years of hard work.

One summer afternoon, while the old samurai gave his lessons, a man approached the group looking for trouble. It was a young warrior with a bad reputation.

The gossipers say that this young gladiator had become famous for his unscrupulous fighting technique. In each battle, he sought victory through slander and provocation until his adversary became so enraged he made a mistake that cost him the fight.

That afternoon, feeling very confident, he wanted to try his luck against the old samurai.

Despite the opposition of his apprentices, the old samurai accepted the challenge.

The young warrior began to insult the old samurai. As time went by, the abuses got worse: he cursed the samurai's ancestors, threw stones at him, and spit in his face.

The hours passed and the wise samurai remained immovable. At the end of the afternoon, the young warrior gave up. Fed up by the old samurai's composure, he abandoned the fight.

The students then surrounded the samurai and asked him, outraged:

"Master, how could you stand so much?" "Why didn't you respond to the young warrior's provocations with words and your sword?" "Why have you let him humiliate you like this?"

"If someone arrives with a gift and you don't accept it, to whom does the gift belong?" asked the smiling teacher.

"To the person who came to deliver it," an apprentice replied.

"The same applies to rage, insults, and envy," the wise samurai explained. "When we do not accept them, they continue to belong to those who carried them with them."

A Voice of Authority

THE MAKER–ISABEL ALLENDE

Isabel Allende has lived a novel life. With 70 million books sold in forty-five languages, she has become the most widely read Latina writer on the planet. A true *maker*. Her professional life has been full of accolades and achievements. But on her journey to the top she has endured pains worthy of the heroines in her books.

Each stage of her life was marked by an episode that would stay with her forever. When she was just four years old, her father

Isabel Allende and Gaby.

abandoned her. As a young woman, amid her ascending journalistic career, she had to leave her homeland Chile to go into exile as a political refugee and start over in a new land. In her later years, she endured the most difficult period of her life: the death of her daughter Paula after an agonizing year in a coma.

Amid each storm, writing has been her refuge, her catharsis, and sometimes, even her lifeline. She learned how to discover in herself an invincible summer for every winter that life gave her.

I met Isabel to record our interview in a loft in Dallas. The cold of the industrial decorations contrasted with the warmth of my guest. Isabel is one of those women who arrives somewhere and quickly makes everyone feel at home. *Are you married? Single? How long have you worked together?* As a good storyteller, she is curious by nature, and for a moment before the cameras were turned on it felt as if she were the one interviewing us.

One thing that caught my attention is how methodical Isabel is when it comes to writing. Every detail of her creative process is planned. And the start date is no exception.

Every January 8, her lucky day, this disciplined Chilean begins to write her books and locks herself away for months to work without interruption. She starts early in the morning and makes sure that all distractions are out of her reach: there is no phone or email in her writing room. A good luck ritual? Before starting to write, she lights a candle in front of the portraits of her daughter Paula and her grandparents to gain the blessing of their protective spirits.

Gaby: When I read about your detailed ritual on January 8, I was wondering one thing . . . How would Isabel feel on January 7?

Isabel: It's horrifying because I don't know what will happen the next day! I already have everything ready. I have the room where I am going to write free of all the above, I have the dictionaries lined up, and all my research already organized.

Gaby: If you want to start writing before January 8, can you hold off until then?

Isabel: I hold off. I just take notes. On January 8, even if I don't have anything, I write something because it's about getting started.

This same resolve Isabel displays when she begins to write her books appears when she has to make great life decisions. Because of this, she braved all fears of old age and loneliness and dared to end a twenty-eight-year marriage just after her seventieth birthday.

In a span of five days her husband left, they cleared out their house, and they went their separate ways. What Isabel never could have imagined was that love was going to knock on her door again—at age seventy-five when she had resigned herself to spending the rest of her days in the company of her dog and favorite books.

A New York lawyer who had heard her on the radio was captivated and began writing letters every day for five months until they finally met in person. The crush was instantaneous. Three days after meeting, he proposed marriage.

Gaby: Isabel, you recount your life so naturally . . . but none of this is normal! (Laughs)

Isabel: (Laughs) I know it's a bit abnormal. Especially at our age. Now, he lives with me with his two bicycles. We are in the same room along with the dog, all under one roof.

Gaby: And what did you think about the idea of marriage?

Isabel: Look, before my mother died, she asked me to get married. According to her, that way I would be protected. I explained that I know how to protect myself and take care of myself. And then she said one of her usual sayings: "Look mijita.' Lovers leave, but husbands stay." (Laughs)

A CLOSER LOOK

Do you want to enjoy the complete conversation between Gaby and Isabel? Visit www.GabyNatale.com to watch the laughter- and emotion-filled interview. In it you will discover:

- Why Isabel decided to get a divorce after twenty-eight years of marriage and bet on love again.
- Isabel's incredible supernatural experience while taking care of her comatose daughter.
- What mischief got her into trouble when she was translating novels from other authors into Spanish at the beginning of her career.

SOME PRACTICAL SUGGESTIONS TO BE A MODEL MAKER OF THE TWENTY-FIRST CENTURY

- *Be a connector between people.* Contrary to what many insecure people believe, opening the door for others will not make you lose opportunities. Only those who have a mindset of scarcity believe that the progress of others means setbacks for them. Don't be mean. Trust that there will be abundance for everyone. Think that every person you have helped along the way is a potential ally. Over time, you will discover that all those people whom you have benefited have become an invaluable network of contacts that may be the key to your next step. Today for you, tomorrow for me.

- *Cultivate your curiosity.* If you're one of those who think that you're "already done" once you have an academic degree, you're in trouble. The skills demanded by the labor market are constantly changing, and it's essential to stay up to date with the changes in your industry. Depending on your profession, many of the things you learned in the classroom may have become obsolete by the time you can start looking for work.

- One of the most extreme examples is what happens to candidates seeking work at Google. The human resources department of the technology giant decided years ago to stop evaluating candidates based mainly on their school or degree. After extensive research, they concluded that what best defines candidates is their ability to adapt, to change, and to learn new skills.

- *Many heads are better than one.* The makers of the last century were convinced that they knew everything, and they rarely listened to others. Especially if those others came with new issues or untested ideas. The companies and makers who will succeed in the new century are those who dare to collaborate, test new formulas—and particularly, those who constantly test their hypotheses. They know that the day they stop doing so they will die out.

- *Be especially generous with those having a hard time.* Those of us who have experienced unemployment or a financial crisis in our lives keep a special place in our hearts for those who held out a hand when we needed it most. It's true that there are ungrateful people who bite the hand that feeds them. But they are exceptions. Don't let the ingratitude of a few steal your desire to help. Most people affectionately remember those who made it easier for them to meet a new contact, who gave them information in the middle of a job search, and who selflessly spent an hour of their time advising them.

- *Apologize.* If at some point in your path the pressures, weakness, or personal insecurity turned you into an "ill-mannered maker," don't think that it's too late to redeem yourself. Perhaps you hurt those around you, or you didn't give someone a chance even though they deserved it. If you are genuinely sorry, call the person you may have hurt and say so. Maybe the person will forgive you, maybe not, but you'll know that at least you did your part. There are few things more healing than making peace with the past.

- *Build your own part-time business.* Life is always changing, and we must be prepared. Relationships or jobs that were once your source of well-being may disappear overnight. One way you can be better prepared when hard times hit is by having a separate activity that makes you extra money. There are a lot of options online for all types of businesses and self-employment. In the next box I suggest opportunities you can start taking advantage of today.

LET'S GET TO WORK:
Getting Started on Your Dreams
Co$$$t Money (Some Ideas to Earn Extra Cash)

Maybe you need some extra capital to start putting your dream into action: taking classes, getting certified for new skills, or buying materials or equipment. Where can you get that much-needed additional cash? It's possible that it's closer than you think . . . maybe even right under your nose!

There has never been an easier time to make extra money independently. Here are some ideas to grow your bank account step by step on your own terms.

- Offer your skills online: sign up on freelance employment sites to offer your skills online. There are markets for many professions, including designers, writers, virtual assistants, illustrators, and even in customer service. There are also websites where you can register as a tutor and host virtual classes to help schoolchildren.

- Sell on classified ad sites: if you have a retail business or unused items in your home that can be converted into money, you can multiply your sales by also offering them online. If you don't know how to design a webpage, don't worry. You can set up your store on the Internet through eBay, Craigslist, MercadoLibre, or on the available classified sites in your country. This can make you money even if you dedicate as little as one day a week to it. You can publish new items and mail the ones you sold in the previous seven days at the same time.

- Take advantage of your knowledge in home repairs: if you know any trades (like plumbing or electrical) or have skills that are useful for home repairs, you can also offer your services online by creating a Thumbtack profile. It's time to monetize home repairs!

- Get behind the wheel in your free time: sign up to be a driver with Uber, Lyft, or some other driving service. This is a job you can do by choosing your own days and schedules. If instead of a car you have a truck, there are opportunities for you too. Some services (such as UShip.com) pay drivers to help them with their parcel delivery orders.

- Rent a room . . . or your entire house: how about making money while on vacation? More and more people rent their home or a room in their home through services such as Airbnb. The advantage of this form of income is that you earn money with what you already have.

- Turn your hobbies into profit: if you're good at creating unique things like handicrafts or custom crafts, there's an online market for you. Through sites like Etsy and Amazon Handmade you can set up virtual stores and sell your creations around the world. Customers on these platforms are looking for original and unique items, so you may be able to charge a little more than usual.

- Look for funding for independent projects: if you have a project in mind but need financing, try publishing it on crowdfunding or micromanagement sites such as IndieGogo, Kickstarter, GoFundMe, or Fondeadora. These platforms allow you to share your project with the world. Then anyone who wants to support you can make a small donation.

- Create online courses: develop courses on the Internet and market them through learning platforms such as Udemy, Coursera, Teachable, or Next University. On these platforms there are people teaching everything from guitar to video editing to public speaking. Professional teachers and amateur instructors coexist and sell their courses independently. The average amount earned by online course authors is $7,000 a year.

- Digital books: maybe the time has come to make money with those stories you write in your spare time and never

dared to publish. Or maybe it's time to take pictures of
your favorite dishes and compile those recipes from
grandma that were kept under lock and key for
generations. If you like to write, you can now publish
and sell your own books even if you don't have a
publishing house. Amazon or Nook digital platforms
allow you to offer your work independently.

TIPS FOR CARING FOR YOUR MAKER SELF

In this section, I would like to explain the relationship between *the Virtuous Circle* and the people around you.

The Virtuous Circle is personal and non-transferable. And there is a very powerful reason for this: nobody but you can decide what makes you really happy. Only you know the motivations that have led you to begin this process and what you expect to get from it. So nobody can tell you how or when you should go through it.

It's an experience that cannot and should not depend on the approval of others. When meeting other people's expectations becomes a constant source of dissatisfaction, disobedience is not a defect. It's a prerequisite for happiness. If you are living your life according to the wishes or mandates of others, make *the Virtuous Circle* your declaration of independence.

As you begin your personal transformation hand in hand with the maker, those around you will notice the changes you are making. It's possible that your thoughts, routines, plans, and even your priorities will change. Don't be surprised if people around you start to have their own opinions about what you're doing!

It's important to be prepared to get varied reactions from those around you. Some will motivate you on this new path, others will be confused and may need more time to understand what is happening. You'll find some who have not the slightest interest in what you are doing, as well as those who will ridicule or envy you. Don't be alarmed. All these reactions are human and natural. When you move through *the Virtuous Circle* you are beginning to win over yourself, and that can sometimes rock people's worlds.

Some of the people around you will have strong reactions to your changes. You will find *allies* wanting to help you in this new path, and you will also encounter others who will try to discourage you. We will call the latter *negatives*. It's good that you identify each of them clearly and be ready to anticipate their reactions. This way, you will know how to better cope with any situations that arise.

IDENTIKIT FOR ALLIES

- They are delighted that you have decided to start your personal transformation and want to support you in the process.
- They believe in your potential and motivate you to move forward. They are your companions on this adventure.
- They help you regain your courage and maintain faith in yourself in your moments of weakness. Allies don't always tell you that everything you do is fantastic; they also often disagree with you.
- If they need to criticize you, they do it with care so as not to hurt your feelings—and only if they believe their observation can help you grow.
- You know you are in front of one because when you finish talking with an ally you feel energized and optimistic.

IDENTIKIT FOR THE NEGATIVES

- They have strong negative feelings about your personal transformation.
- Their reactions can be triggered by skepticism, ignorance, or because your transformation threatens them.
- They focus their attention mostly on the problems, difficulties, or disadvantages that could result from your transformation.
- They don't have the ability to see your potential—or worse, they see it and choose to minimize it.
- After spending time with them, you feel overwhelmed or drained.

Make a mental map of the people around you and identify those who have the potential to become your greatest allies. Recruit them and share your dreams with them. It's important that you make them part of your adventure and that they help you stay strong on this path.

Let me save you the suspense: there are going to be moments in your journey through *the Virtuous Circle* when you're going to feel weak or disoriented. Your strength and enthusiasm will be tested. That is when you will need support from your allies the most. No one who has truly gone far has done so without a team.

If you discover among your closest companions some negatives, don't get frustrated. They all have the right to their own opinion. Don't tire yourself out trying to convince them. Just stay focused on your path. The doors you are looking for will require all your energy to open. Be efficient and use it on worthwhile tasks.

It's also important that you take a minute before giving someone the title of *negative*. Sometimes, instead of bad people, what we see are good people in bad moments. Either way, don't take it personally. Remember that the reactions of others are just that: of others.

DO IT ANYWAY[2]

People are often unreasonable, irrational and self-centered.
Forgive them anyway.
If you are kind, people may accuse you of selfish, ulterior motives.
Be kind anyway.
If you are successful, you will win some unfaithful friends and some genuine enemies.
Succeed anyway.
If you are honest and sincere, people may deceive you.
Be honest and sincere anyway.
What you spend years creating, others could destroy overnight.
Create anyway.
If you find serenity and happiness, some may be jealous.
Be happy anyway.
The good you do today, will often be forgotten.
Do good anyway.
Give the best you have, and it may never be enough.
Give your best anyway.

—MOTHER TERESA OF CALCUTTA

• • •

In the First Person

We Are All Connected—
The Story of Nelva, My Grandmother and Ally

In this chapter, I wanted to share stories that had to do with how deep and complex the connections between people can be.

The story that closes this chapter is dedicated to my grandmother Nelva who, despite being from another generation, was always a great ally in my follies and adventures.

✄

Sometimes, we can't even imagine how deeply we are connected to each other. The last few years of Nelva's life helped me understand how love can open communication channels even in the most unexpected circumstances.

I was always a very spoiled granddaughter. Nelva was not only my grandmother but also my ally. She loved me and showed it to me all the time: she indulged me by baking my favorite cornstarch *alfajores*, embroidered my name by hand in my preschool uniform, gave me impromptu knitting classes, and even became my secret accomplice by making for me the crafts I had to turn in at school. When I was a girl, sleeping over at my grandmother's house was (to me) the best!

As I grew up, my grandmother and I continued to have a very nice relationship. Despite my many moves (first to other cities and then to other countries), we were always in touch, loving each other at a distance. We talked on the phone often, and every time I visited Argentina, I always made time to go see her and surprise her with flowers or her favorite snacks from the bakery La Paris.

Every time I saw her, she asked me her (somewhat indiscreet) favorite question: "Are you and your husband still in love?" I answered yes between laughs, amused by her quip. Once satisfied, she always said the same thing to me: "What joy! The only important thing is love, the *only* important thing is love."

The goodbyes at the end of each trip always left a lump in my throat. I knew well that one day that "Until next time, Abu!"[3] I was trying to make sound cheerful and casual would become the last goodbye.

After turning eighty, Grandma Nelva's health started to deteriorate faster. First it was her hands. Those fingers that had been able to embroider, knit, and cook with total mastery began to tremble. So she was forced to stop doing the hobbies she enjoyed so much.

Then it was her legs. She barely had the strength to stand. One day she fell, broke her hip, and could no longer walk.

During the last visits, I realized that my grandmother was different: sadness had taken over her. Seeing herself in a wheelchair had been a major blow. She was ashamed to have to ask for help and depend on others. As much as her children and grandchildren sought to encourage her, she no longer felt the same desire to do things. Not even my stories could make her smile.

Soon she developed Alzheimer's disease. She began to have bouts of forgetfulness and confusion. There were days when she was lost in time and space. I kept calling her as usual, but the conversations were no longer the same. Nelva no longer asked me questions. She got tired after a few minutes on the phone. What used to be conversations had now become monologues. But I felt that calling her was still worthwhile, because it's always nice to hear from the people you love.

It was remarkable that, even in her worst Alzheimer's moments, she never forgot who I was. Her mind played tricks on her but not when it came to me. Months could go by without us seeing each other in person, but when they told her she had a call from her granddaughter, she spoke to me with absolute certainty: "Hello, Gaby!" And without missing a beat: "Are you and your husband still in love? Love is the only important thing!"

One day, her fragile body failed her. She had a stroke that left her in a coma. The doctors explained that my grandmother was in a state of deep unconsciousness. She could no longer speak or respond to stimuli. The poor woman was hostage to a cruel dream that left her caught between life and death. "She no longer understands anything that happens around her," the specialists warned.

There were plenty of well-meaning people who wanted to protect me and recommended that I not go see her. They warned me that Nelva was very frail, that perhaps it would be better to keep the memories of her glory days. I wanted to visit her anyway. I brought her perfume and Hinds Lotion, her favorite.

When I arrived at the hospital, I hardly recognized her. Connected to machines that monitored vital functions was someone who barely looked like my grandmother. Her delicate little hands, which always had painted red nails, were now tied to a board and battered by arthritis. Her flirtatious hair, which she had always been careful to keep blonde and wavy, was now silver and combed straight back. Even her mouth had changed shape now that she no longer had her false teeth in.

I approached her bed and stared at her. She was sleeping peacefully. I knew that this moment alone would be the last between us. The final farewell had arrived.

I took her arm gently and began to speak loudly. I told her that I felt very grateful to have had her as a grandmother, that I loved her very much, and that I felt very fortunate to have met her.

I paused to swallow and make sure my voice didn't crack. I wanted to be careful so that she felt only my love and not my anguish. I told her that I had been very happy every time we were together. I thanked her for every embroidery, every recipe, and every birthday we shared.

Suddenly, as I spoke, the expression on her face changed. Her relaxed eyelids contracted and began to blink. Her mouth, which had remained motionless, began to move up and down without stopping, as if trying to mumble something.

The intensity of her movements was in direct proportion to the emotional charge of what I was telling her. If I told her that the day was sunny, her face would relax. If I was moved and told her how much I loved her, her face tensed.

I knew that even in her state of unconsciousness my grandmother had received that last farewell message.

The doctors may not agree with me, but I know what I experienced that day. She, from her coma, and I, by her bed, had managed to connect.

Perhaps the key to understanding the unintelligible is precisely the phrase she always repeated to me:

The only important thing is love.

CHAPTER 5

THE APPRENTICE: PERFECT YOUR DREAM

We are what we repeatedly do.
Excellence, then, is not an act, but a habit.

—WILL DURANT[1]

#VirtuousCircle

Ideas

HAVE NO AGE.

@GabyNatale

Take a photo and share it online using
#VirtuousCircle

T he apprentice is the fourth archetype of *the Virtuous Circle*. The apprentice tells you that the time has arrived to become extraordinarily good at what you do. The apprentice will guide you in the sublime task of transforming yourself into your own masterpiece.

Together, you will be able to polish the talents and skills you need to achieve your dream. Through your personal transformation, you will simultaneously become a sculptor and a sculpture.

Your apprentice self reminds you of your own unlimited possibilities: what is not today, may be tomorrow. With the apprentice's help, you can perfect what you visualized with the dreamer, planned with the architect, and began to put into action with the maker.

Through the apprentice's example of naïveté, we learn that excellence is not a goal, but a constant pursuit: Only those willing to be an eternal apprentice can aspire to one day become a master. That is why great geniuses and innovators have always retained an apprentice state of mind.

Those who declare themselves apprentices open the door of knowledge by recognizing their ignorance. Those who declare themselves experts open the door of ignorance by blindly trusting in their knowledge.

Being an apprentice does not elevate or degrade your status. An apprentice isn't better than anyone and no one is better than the apprentice.

The apprentice is a novice, but not submissive. Shutting up and obeying blindly is not part of the apprentice's nature. Apprentices' greatness lies in having the humility to constantly question their own knowledge to give birth to improved versions of themselves and their work.

The most astute learners are those who have mastered the art of receiving and releasing knowledge as needed in their evolution or creative process. How could Pablo Picasso have founded Cubism if he had not first *embraced* the classic painting and drawing principles of realism? How could Pablo Picasso have founded Cubism if he had not *released* the classical principles of painting and drawing of realism?

It's in this constant dance between learning and unlearning that apprentices find their own voice.

Good apprentices manage their own learning. They know that the path to wisdom isn't always linear. They take it for granted that there will be successes and failures. But they are convinced that the seed of the next lesson they need to learn is found in each back-and-forth. Remember that to advance on the path to mastery all teachers must first embrace their inner apprentice.

In This Chapter You Will Find

- The section "Fixed Mindset vs. Growth Mindset."
- Do you think that talent can be cultivated, or are you one of those people who are convinced you are born with it? Think about it, because you will discover that how you answer can have transcendental consequences for your future development and success.
- "The Japanese Philosophy of *Kaizen*." Discover the revolutionary power of continual small changes to improve your life.

- The segment "In the First Person: From the Carpet Warehouse to the Red Carpet (part 1)," a story in which I will share with you the rough start to my television show *SuperLatina*. You will see why this stage became an accelerated program of ingenuity for this apprentice writing to you today.
- An insightful conversation with bestselling author Don Miguel Ruiz for all the apprentices who would love to learn how to make better use of ancient wisdom in our modern lives.

IS TALENT BORN OR MADE? FIXED MINDSET VS. GROWTH MINDSET

Since the beginning of time, philosophers and thinkers have debated whether the human qualities we most admire, such as intelligence and charisma, are virtues we are born with or if we cultivate them through learning.

Is it possible to develop, through pure effort, capacities we were not born with?

That is precisely the question psychologist Carol S. Dweck asked in her book *Mindset: The New Psychology of Success*. In her acclaimed work, the psychologist from Stanford University distinguishes between two attitudes that affect our chances of success: the fixed mindset and the growth mindset.

•   •   •

Fixed mindset

The fixed mindset considers that personal qualities are immutable. People with this mindset are convinced that their intelligence and talent are set at birth. They believe that the mix of virtues and defects they are born with are what they will carry with them for the rest of their lives. Basically, you are either good or you are not. That's it.

Those with a fixed mindset have a deep need to prove to themselves over and over again that they are capable of doing this or the other. Since they are convinced that each person only has "a certain amount of talent" it's essential for them to prove that they belong to the select group that has come to the world with exceptional gifts.

With a fixed mindset people put their egos at stake in every challenge they face. There's a powerful reason why they do it: if they fail, it will be clear that they are impostors and didn't have the talent to live up to the circumstances. That's why people with a fixed mindset feel vulnerable when things don't go as planned. They avoid situations where they may be at risk of making a mistake. According to their binary way of seeing reality, an error unmasks them to the world, exposing them as "losers."

Identikit of Those Who Live with a Fixed Mindset
- They avoid challenges.
- They give up too soon.
- They think that effort is worthless.
- They reject all criticisms and consider them useless.
- They feel threatened by the triumphs of others.

Growth mindset

The opposite of the fixed mindset is the growth mindset. Those who adopt a growth mindset are convinced that talent and skills can be cultivated through effort. They argue that it's impossible to know a person's potential in advance. The only sure way to discover it is through years of learning, discipline, and self-improvement.

They have a dynamic vision of talent and intelligence: it is not all or nothing. Whether they're good or bad at something depends on the specific task and time allotted. For those who adopt a growth mindset, failing is not a terrible thing. It's simply a necessary part of learning.

Unlike those with a fixed mindset, for those with a growth mindset, no failure completely defines their ability or who they are. In short, they can always improve. They know that with time and dedication they will be able to cultivate the skills they need and will see progress.

"Today I didn't do very well, but if I try hard, it's possible that tomorrow will be much better for me"—this phrase that would summarize their way of seeing life very well.

People who have a growth mindset want to push their own limits. They bloom in the face of adversity. They become eternal apprentices.

Identikit of Those Who Live with a Growth Mindset
- They enjoy challenges.
- They persevere when they encounter obstacles.
- They consider that effort is required to achieve excellence.
- They learn from criticism.
- They are inspired by the triumphs of others.

SELF-FULFILLING PROPHECIES

According to Dweck, one of the most surprising things is that both fixed and growth mindsets have premises that can become self-fulfilling prophecies for those who adopt them. As a result, both the supporters of the fixed mindset and the growth mindset end up confirming their own hypotheses with their behaviors.

Those who live with a fixed mindset are more likely to abandon a project or task when the first signs of difficulty arrive. Because they are afraid of failing, they prefer not to expose themselves to failure and will conclude that it's better not to keep trying. This way, they will also confirm what they thought: their abilities are set and trying to acquire new ones makes no sense.

Those who adopt a growth mindset also confirm their own conviction that it's possible to develop talent and become extraordinarily good at something through effort. As they see results, they attribute it to their dedication and thus confirm that talent can be something that develops with effort and discipline.

In short, in the face of adversity:

- Those with a fixed mindset give up. Their failure is proof that they ultimately had nothing valuable to offer the world. As a result, they limit their own growth and develop a deterministic view of the world.
- Those who have a growth mindset grow. They strive to improve everything they can. If they succeed, they rejoice. If they fail, they take it as a part of the learning process that will make them even better. As a result, they feel they have more control over their destinies. They become eternal apprentices and never stop growing.

The good news is those who have a *fixed mindset* can work to consciously develop a *growth mindset*. According to Dweck, the beliefs you choose about yourself will profoundly affect your future performance and can be a determining factor in achieving your dreams.

GAME: Tell Me What Saying You Use . . . and I'll Tell You What Kind of Mindset You Have!

Words are extremely powerful. We use popular phrases and aphorisms every day without even thinking about it. We grew up with them; they're embedded in our minds. We use these phrases almost automatically. But many of them express different types of mindsets.

Here are some examples:

- "A leopard can't change its spots" (fixed mindset).
- "You can't make a silk purse out of a sow's ear" (fixed).
- "God helps those who help themselves" (growth mindset . . . with divine help!).
- "The darkest hour comes before the dawn" (the fixed mindset's response to the previous saying).
- "You will reap what you sow" (growth mindset).
- "The poet is born, not made" (fixed mindset).

SOME PRACTICAL SUGGESTIONS TO DEVELOP A GROWTH MINDSET

- *Learn something new in a field you're not certain you are good in:* People with a fixed mindset have a strong preference for only doing things they already know they are good at, since they have a constant fear of failure.

That fear, however, is a behavior we develop as we grow. Children are not like that. They love to learn and enjoy trying new things. No children who have gotten into trouble for drawing on the walls of their house did it because they wanted to create the best children's mural in the world. They were just having so much fun coloring that when they ran out of paper . . . they continued coloring on the wall! That's the mindset that we have to recover as adults (of course without getting into trouble with walls or anything else).

One way to exercise the growth mindset is to encourage yourself to do something new, something you don't know how well you will do in. The idea is to enjoy learning, beyond the result. It's also to understand that there's no reason to be alarmed if something requires more work than you imagined or doesn't work out the first time you try. It's simply a part of the learning process.

- *Declare your defiance against stereotypes.* The world is full of stereotypes or "little signs" that we, more or less, consciously hang around one another's necks.

If he's studious, he can't be good at sports.

If she's blonde and attractive, of course she will never win a Nobel Prize in astronomy!

If you're over fifty years old, of course you don't understand anything about computers. And forget about starting a relationship at your age, because you have already had several failed ones already. You're not someone who anyone could seriously consider starting a family with.

People have also hung signs on you based on your gender or the social group you come from. Similarly, you may have hung one on someone else without even realizing it.

How do you deal with those little signs? How much do they condition your life every day? Have you stopped doing something important just because it was an activity that supposedly didn't fit people who carried a sign like yours?

Believing what those little signs say about you is one of the most destructive acts of self-sabotage you can commit. First, because what the signs say are not your own vision but something created by someone else. Second, because those little signs describe a static and immovable world. (If someone is good at X, then they can't be good at Y. These are examples of a fixed mindset.) And finally, because those little signs are based on opinions, not facts.

In short, each little sign is a static version of someone else's opinion about you or people like you. Why base the expectations you have of your own capacity on something arbitrary and external?

- *Reprogram your way of seeing failures and mistakes.* Do you think that the only thing worthwhile is winning? If your team doesn't finish first and is instead the runner-up, do you react more harshly than if you had been in last place? Maybe it's time to rethink the way you process your own and others' failures and mistakes!

Someone who thinks only in terms of winning and losing does not take into account a very important part of the equation: the progress made.

In a soccer match, a shot that just misses, that hits the goalpost, can be interpreted in several ways. For a coach with a fixed mindset, who only understands the final score, it will be just like any other missed shot, even the ones that weren't close. On the other hand, a shrewd coach with a growth mindset will see that missed shot as the key to improving tactics. With a little luck and hard work that miss may become a great goal in the next game.

Similarly, you may be very close to scoring a goal in something that interests you, but you have a little bit more work left before you do. It's possible, for example, that you haven't been able to pass the entrance exam just *yet*. Or that you haven't passed that difficult audition just *yet* either. Perhaps your grades are still the equivalent of "a ball that hit the goalpost." But if you manage to get better with each attempt, you have a reason to be optimistic. Sometimes we are so focused on the end result, that we miss the hidden treasure that develops inside us as we overcome obstacles.

- *Use the triumphs of others to inspire you.* If you believe that the triumphs of others minimize your own achievements, the time has come to make a mental readjustment. What others do, whether good or bad, says nothing about you. It only applies only to them.

  Think about this example for a moment. If your neighbor starts running the New York City Marathon and places first, will his performance make you less agile than you are now? If he or she comes in last, do you think that will magically turn you into a great runner? Only your own effort and dedication will determine your agility, regardless of how many marathons your neighbor runs.

  There is a much more productive way of thinking about the triumphs of others: turn them into irrefutable testimony that something incredible can be achieved.

WHY SHOULD WE
BECOME ETERNAL APPRENTICES?

There are three main reasons why I believe that adopting an apprentice's attitude permanently is one of the best things you can do for yourself.

Reason #1: For Your Vitality

More and more people are living longer, fuller lives. In industrialized countries, the life expectancy is almost eighty years. Thanks to advances in medicine, an increasingly large percentage of those eight decades of life takes place independently and actively. Becoming an eternal apprentice means rethinking your own aging process. How would your life change if you thought about the passing years as an opportunity for constant learning instead of anticipating a downward slide to decrepitude? What would happen if the passing years went hand in hand with permanent personal, social, and intellectual development?

Today, older adults enjoy more years of mobility, social life, romantic life . . . and even sex! In previous generations these benefits would have been considered science fiction. If you think about it, sixty- to eighty-year-old people today are very different from their parents or grandparents at the same age.

Being an apprentice teaches us a great lesson: the passage of time is inevitable, but growth is optional. A lot of your ability to be happy is going to depend on your decision to actively work on improving your well-being. In the decades ahead, having a mindset of constant improvement and embracing your inner apprentice is the key to living your life to the fullest.

Reason #2: For Your Career

The workplace and its demands are constantly changing. The era is past when a worker would peacefully spend all of their productive years in the same company and move up with promotion after promotion until they retired from that same company.

Technological advances, businesses being sold, and labor being exported to more competitive countries, among other factors, make working conditions more unstable than in previous generations. Reinventing yourself professionally not once but several times has gone from being the exception to being the rule.

The next wave of change is coming. The ones who cling to old formulas and who don't have the flexibility to seek out constant learning run the risk of being held hostage by skills that have become obsolete.

The technology has already been developed so that anyone who goes to a supermarket can buy their merchandise without human assistance. Pretty soon, thanks to an app on your phone, your entire shopping trip will be done without even getting in a checkout line. Amazon Go was the first initiative of this kind and has the potential to eliminate all cashier jobs on the planet.

This is not the only example of new technologies performing tasks currently done by human beings. In the area of heavy manufacturing, robots are replacing workers and performing most of the tasks humans used to do. In the transportation industry, the development of self-driving cars and trucks is advancing. Fast food restaurant chains are testing out smart kiosks for customers to place their order and receive their food without the need for human interaction. Even in industries associated with creativity, such as journalism and advertising, early versions of programs that totally or partially automate writing articles or editing videos are being tested.

All of these changes will dramatically affect the number of jobs available to twenty-first-century professionals. A joint report by Citi and the University of Oxford recently pointed out that in industrialized countries 57 percent of jobs are at risk of being totally or partially replaced by automation.

Some specialists believe that artificial intelligence and automation will have the same devastating effect on middle class jobs that the Industrial Revolutions had on the working class. The difference is that while the Industrial Revolutions took centuries to reduce the number of workers needed on assembly lines, the technological transformations ahead have the capacity to be introduced on a global scale in a matter of decades.

Over the next few years, becoming an eternal apprentice will increasingly be a matter of survival, not preference.

The good news is that if you develop an apprentice attitude and anticipate these changes by honing your talent for what is coming, you will be in an excellent position to create new business opportunities and take advantage of the new work scenario.

Reason #3: For Your Creativity

There is something that an eternal apprentice is clear about: *Ideas have no age.*

It's never too early or too late to fight for your dreams. The history of the world is full of early genius and late success. People who trust in their capacity and embrace constant learning can transcend their chronological age.

Banish the idea of imposing an "expiration date" on yourself just because you have reached a certain age. As the decades go by your physical performance may start facing some limitations, but for those who remain curious and active, creative performance can be unlimited. *There is absolutely no reason why the "youngest" ideas cannot come from those who have spent the most time on this planet.*

Forget about whether you're too young or too old. The most important thing is that you take advantage of the time you have by becoming an increasingly better version of yourself.

At a certain point in my life, I was always the youngest person in meetings at work. Sometimes, I felt so insecure that I didn't have the confidence to share my ideas. That's why I felt especially frustrated when I found out that someone with more experience than me was congratulated for saying the *exact* same thing that I hadn't shared! It took me some time to learn that, although I had less experience than the rest of the team, my opinion was still valuable. If I had focused my attention more on my creative ability, instead of worrying about my age, I would have spared myself quite a few self-loathing sleepless nights.

So don't stop. Trust in your greatness. Your creativity has no age.

The Minute Before Suicide: Harland's Story

Harland was sixty-five years old, had just retired, and was so depressed that just thinking about suicide eased his pain. He felt that after working his entire life he had achieved almost nothing he set out to do when he was young. He was ashamed to feel that he was reaching the last years of his life and had so little to show the world and himself.

He looked back on his life and felt that it was marked by failure. He was fatherless by the age of five. By sixteen he had to abandon his studies. At eighteen he had gotten married and had a daughter, only to get divorced two years later and lose custody of his little girl.

He spent most of his life jumping from job to job without much success. He had tried his luck as an insurance salesman, lamp merchant, and tire dealer. He had failed in every attempt to better himself.

Why continue living when he had failed so many times?

In the midst of the darkness, Harland had a lucid moment that made him reconsider his decision to take his own life. He realized that despite being discouraged he still wanted to do things. And there was something that he was extremely good at: he knew how to cook better than anyone else.

The kitchen had always been his oasis amid the pain. He learned as a child to help his mother after she was widowed, but he enjoyed preparing food tremendously. Maybe it was worth staying alive so he could cook.

He borrowed eighty-seven dollars and bought a fryer. He developed a unique recipe for cooking chicken and began selling it door-to-door in a town in Kentucky.

The rest is history. That sixty-five-year-old man who had wanted to commit suicide was the founder of Kentucky Fried Chicken, one of the most famous fast food chains on the planet with a presence in more than a hundred countries.

Harland became known worldwide as "Colonel Sanders" and today his image is part of the company logo. Before he died, Colonel Sanders revealed what he believed was the secret of his success:

"I've only had two rules: do everything you can and do it the best you can. It's the only way you'll achieve great things in life."

A Voice of Authority

THE APPRENTICE—
DON MIGUEL RUIZ

"Is it possible to learn without teachers?" I asked Don Miguel Ruiz enthusiastically as soon as I got him on the phone.

"Of course, Gaby!" The bestselling author of *The Four Agreements* replied optimistically.

"In fact, my friend, not only is it possible, I would say that it's necessary. We can all be our own shaman. The first rule is to discard the conditions others want to impose on you based on their own experience."

And boy has he done it!

Apprentice-by-excellence, shaman, Nagual,[2] surgeon, author, and survivor of two tragedies that almost cost him his life. All these titles, and many more, fit Don Miguel Ruiz, the renowned maker of numerous personal growth bestsellers, including the classic *The Four Agreements*.

Don Miguel Ruiz was born on the outskirts of Guadalajara. He was the youngest of thirteen in a humble home full of ancestral wisdom. His parents were respected figures in the town where he grew up. His mother was a healer, and his father was recognized as a "nahual," a word that is used in Toltec mythology to describe someone who has healing powers.

Don Miguel learned the spirit of service from his parents, a calling that would initially lead him to complete his medical studies and then practice as a surgeon for several decades.

Western science and medicine would be the formative stage of his life. The next step for this apprentice would be, ironically, that of "unlearning."

His unlearning process began, literally, by accident. After a car crash that almost cost him his life, Don Miguel spent a great deal of time in recovery. There, facing his own fears and limitations, he understood that Western medicine was effective in curing the "matter," the human body, but that it didn't take into account the other part of the equation: vital energy.

Having learned this lesson, Don Miguel made the most drastic decision of his career: he decided to quit his job as a surgeon and return to his roots. He recalled the ancient Toltec wisdom that his parents had taught him as a child, and he realized that these teachings were the complement to his scientific training.

Near the tenth anniversary of the accident that changed his life, Don Miguel sat down to write his first book. In three months, he finished *The Four Agreements*.

Twenty years later, and with four million copies sold, I asked Don Miguel what was the greatest lesson he learned from reversing gears like this. His response amazed me:

"The problem with learning is that sometimes we allow society to condition our learning. For example, society teaches us to love with conditions, which is the most selfish form of love: I love you if you allow me to control you. But since everyone wants the same thing, we end up internalizing that way of loving in our relationship with ourselves. From there comes conditional self-esteem: we allow ourselves to love ourselves as long as we meet the expectations others have placed on us. We love ourselves with conditions: I love myself if people appreciate me, love me, respect me, admire me, fear me. Love is the opposite. Love must be unconditional. The only way to exercise healthy self-esteem is to accept ourselves as we are. Acceptance is the only necessary condition of love."

Before saying goodbye, he shared an unforgettable quote with me about the value of becoming eternal apprentices:

"To be good learners we must accept our ignorance and open ourselves to learning without conditions. In love, and in learning, everything goes."

A Closer Look

If you want to listen to the rest of the conversation, including his point-by-point explanation about how to apply his four agreements to our daily lives, don't miss my interview with Don Miguel Ruiz on my podcast at www.GabyNatale.com.

"KAIZEN-IZING" OUR LIFE: "TODAY BETTER THAN YESTERDAY, TOMORROW BETTER THAN TODAY"

The other day in a café, I overheard an intimate conversation between three best friends. One of the friends confessed that she had met a new beau and felt she was living the fullest romance of her life. She was already planning a romantic weekend trip. Another proudly mentioned that she had signed up to study Italian at the university. She loved the opera and wanted to be able to sing her favorite songs . . . even if it was only in the shower! As they told jokes, the third friend reminded the others that before saying goodbye they should take a "selfie" to immortalize the moment. Then they could upload the photo to social media.

"Smile, because we're getting better and better every time! We don't even need filters!" one of the three exclaimed saucily.

As I watched them leave the café, I was delighted with the vibrant spirit of this group of friends. What fascinated me the most was that these youthful "girls" who had entertained me so much . . . were over seventy years old!

Even without trying, they were perfect examples of *kaizen* 改善—the Japanese philosophy that proposes constant improvement as a way of life.

The word *kaizen* 改善 is composed of the words *kai* (change) and *zen* (well). Those who follow *kaizen* as a spiritual doctrine are convinced that our life (work, social, or family) deserves to be constantly perfected. *If I came into this world and I am alive, it is to be better and better every time.*

The origins of *kaizen* date back to mid-twentieth-century Japan. After being defeated in World War II, Japan faced a bleak future: its economy was in crisis, two of its cities had been ravaged by atomic bombs, the population was demoralized, and they had limited natural resources.

Amid such a pitiful situation, how could this small island reverse its fate? *Kaizen* emerged as an attempt by Japanese companies to answer that question.

Instead of lamenting their bad fortune, Japanese business leaders decided to focus their energies on developing manufacturing processes that would drive the constant, gradual, and orderly improvement of their factories. The idea was to take maximum advantage of the few resources they had.

With ingenuity, they created improvement mechanisms that eliminated waste, trained staff, and optimized the use of time. The ultimate goal? To change continually in order to become better every day.

The implementation of the *kaizen* yielded some surprising results. In a couple of decades, Japan went from suffering miserably to becoming an economic superpower. Between 1960 and 1980, the country's economic growth was so extraordinary that historians baptized this period "The Japanese Miracle."

Since then, *kaizen* spread beyond the field of business. The principles of constant improvement were adopted as a philosophy of life and led followers to ask themselves a transcendental question: *Why not love ourselves enough to work on our well-being and self-improvement every day?*

It's possible that this is one of the most transformative questions we can ask ourselves.

The Deming Cycle

One of the most used tools in *kaizen* is called the "Deming Cycle," developed by W. Edwards Deming, considered the father of quality control. It proposes a strategy of continuous quality improvement through the application of four steps: plan, do, verify, and act.

Using the cycle is very simple. The first step is to identify what you want to achieve and establish a plan to achieve it. The second step is to take the actions you planned. The third step is to check that the plan is effective or to make any necessary changes. The fourth step is to compile what you learned in the previous step and put the improvements into action.

At the end of the cycle, the process begins again, incorporating the progress made in the previous cycle.

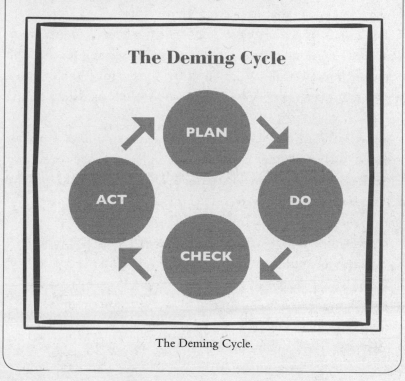

The Deming Cycle.

KAIZEN IN ACTION:
FEEDING HARLEM'S PEOPLE IN NEED

Recently, I found an article in the *New York Times* detailing the implementation of *kaizen* in an unusual space, Food Bank for New York City, the most important charitable organization in the fight against hunger in the United States. It's estimated that Food Bank feeds 1.5 million people in need per year.

In 2013, Food Bank received a very special proposal. Instead of a large check, Toyota decided to donate the advice of its best *kaizen* specialists. The objective? Help them identify areas where they could improve in order to become more efficient.

Food Bank executives were skeptical. How much could a group of Toyota's corporate engineers know about serving food to the homeless in New York? What Food Bank executives didn't know was that Toyota engineers were about to revolutionize their dining rooms.

As established by the Deming cycle, the first step Toyota specialists took was to identify inefficiencies and *plan* processes so that Food Bank could improve its service. They found two key areas that needed to be improved to become more efficient:

- The lines in the dining room were very long. The process had to be more dynamic so that people who needed to eat would wait less.
- The process of assembling food boxes was not properly organized: it required a lot of volunteers, which made the process too lengthy.

Now that they knew what the problem was, the engineers could move on to the second step of the Deming Cycle, *do*. They used the *kaizen* philosophy to introduce small changes that would improve the functioning of the dining rooms:

- They increased the size of the boxes in which they put the food to be transported. Larger boxes reduced the amount of travel needed to move food.
- They introduced the option of "take-out bags" so that those in need could pick up the food and eat it outside Food Bank if they preferred. This way they minimized

the space used in the dining room and shortened wait times for people in line.

- They created shelves marked with different colors depending on the type of food to be stored or served to expedite the filling of bags and the packing of food boxes.

During the third step, *verify*, they reviewed the changes they had made and checked which ones worked best. In the last phase, *act*, the new processes were improved by incorporating all the information they had collected in the previous step.

When they measured the results, the changes were extraordinary:

- In a Harlem dining room, the wait time for a plate of food dropped from ninety to eighteen minutes.
- In the organization's pantry in Staten Island, the time needed to fill bags with food decreased from eleven to five minutes.
- Packing time for food boxes was reduced from three minutes to eleven seconds.

At the end of the experiment, Food Bank executives threw distrust out the window. Thanks to the help of Toyota engineers, they also now swell the ranks of *kaizen* supporters.

Practical Ideas for "*Kaizen*-izing" Your Life

- The first step is to determine the problem and set an objective. What aspect or aspects of your life would you like to make more efficient? Then you have to document where you are and where you would like to be in that area. According to the *kaizen* philosophy, "that which is measured, improves."

- The Japanese call *muda* those processes or activities that don't add value. One of the most common *muda*s is the time taken to get to and from work. According to the United States Census, it takes an average worker fifty minutes to go to and from home (twenty-five minutes each way). What would happen if we could convert that dead time into useful minutes? You could use those fifty minutes to organize your to-do list, make needed calls, or take a virtual class with the help of podcasts or audiobooks. If you consider that a hundred thousand–word novel lasts approximately ten hours in audio format, a conservative calculation would tell us that, using your travel time as a classroom, you could end up finishing a book every twelve to fifteen workdays. In the course of a year that would add up to around fifteen additional books read just by changing the way you use your commute time.

- If you are trying to improve your health, you can apply *kaizen* by creating a calendar with small, but constant, steps. For example, you can start by making a weekly plan that includes taking a healthy homemade lunch to work. If you add a small change like walking ten minutes a day and gradually add five to ten more minutes to your routine, by the end of the year you will see the numbers on the scale go down. Meanwhile, all the lunches outside of the office that you avoided by bringing a healthy homemade lunch will add up to some extra money in the bank. Using a conservative estimate, you would be saving $7 and eliminating about two hundred calories from your diet per day after these changes. Each week, you will have an additional $35 in your pocket and a thousand fewer calories in your diet. In the course of a year that will be 1,820 more dollars and fifty-two thousand fewer calories.

- Eliminating waste and excess is another way forward in the *kaizen*. That's why it's essential to track exactly what you spend money on. Discriminate between necessary and optional expenses. Look at the list objectively and ask yourself if there are ways to manage that money more efficiently. Are there ways to achieve the same or better results using fewer resources? What are the areas of waste? How could these resources be reused in a more positive way? Remember that small, consistent long-term changes also lead to great results in your finances.

- The *kaizen* seeks constant advancement, not perfection. Improved and finished is preferable to perfect. If things progress, you are on the right track. In a while, check again, correct your course if there's a problem, execute the necessary solutions, and start the cycle again.

In the First Person

From the Carpet Warehouse to the Red Carpet (Part 1)

For most television hosts, pre-premiere preparation of their own program involves promotional tours, glamorous photo shoots, and never-ending wardrobe fittings. In my case, the plan was quite different: it included wooden planks, a set of paint rollers, and cans of pink paint.

Before and after. In the photo on the left is yours truly painting the first *SuperLatina* studio inside a carpet warehouse in a shopping center in Odessa, Texas. On the right, many years later, posing on the red carpet of the Latin Billboard Awards.

As you can see in the photo, I had to literally get down to work so that the set of my first show would become a reality. I had no idea that, thanks to that humble roller with pink paint, a new chapter would open that would change my life forever and give this apprentice many lessons and experiences.

Before continuing with this story, let me tell you how I came to have this opportunity.

At that time, I lived in a small Texan city called Midland-Odessa. After having lived in Washington, D.C., and Mexico, I had moved to West Texas. I had been working as a news anchor for several years. I loved my job and the locals were wonderful, but I was at the point where I realized that I had completed a cycle and needed to look for new opportunities.

When you work in front of the camera in a small market, you experience a unique situation: your work has a very high public exposure but very low monetary compensation. The result is an explosive combo: your ego expands while your pocket shrinks. You are popular and spend a significant portion of your time signing autographs and taking pictures with your fans. But that popularity does not translate to money. Just like everyone else, you struggle to save for a down payment on a home.

This unique mix guarantees that you receive the worst of two worlds. You face the lack of privacy problems that celebrities suffer, but you have neither the fortune nor the resources of real stars to solve them. Simply put, you're screwed.

Since your face appears in television advertisements, newspaper advertisements, highway signs, promotional materials, and is even printed on station vehicles, everyone assumes that you lead a life of luxury, but the reality is nothing like that fantasy.

That's why, in small markets, every encounter between the hosts and the audience is a potential disappointment: You never live up to their expectations. They're disappointed to learn that the "Famous Television News Anchor" is their neighbor in a commonplace apartment complex. They are let down when they find you browsing the sales rack beside them in the mall or are surprised when you ask them for help in the parking lot because your old car decided, once again, that it won't start. They could never guess that the "star" they saw every night on television was making only $27,000 per year, about what a waitress makes in the U.S. and hardly enough to make ends meet.

Some television personalities can't tolerate this discrepancy between audience expectations and reality. They bury themselves in debt to pretend to have a social status they can't afford.

Others simply change jobs or markets in order to thrive. I've had colleagues in small markets who have left a job on television to work as oilfield laborers or in a restaurant kitchen, since those paid better than the television station.

As a result of this unusual cross between high profile and low pay, real life tragicomedies occur. I have been the master of ceremonies in charity events to help people in need, just to be confronted by the reality that the beneficiary of the raffle drove a much better car than I!

I have also had an obsessive fan start sending me very scary "love" messages. These are the same type of problems big celebrities face, but unlike them you don't have the budget to hire bodyguards or chauffeurs . . . so you better entrust yourself to the Virgin Mary with all your strength!

In my case, the problem was not just that the salary was low. What made things worse was that my husband and I were paying exorbitant fees and legal bills to obtain permanent residence in the United States.

Our process to obtain residence cards had to start not once or twice . . . but three times! That's why after four long years of paperwork, when our permanent residency was approved, we decided it was time to start our own business. We would launch a television show!

But where do we start? Looking back, not having the slightest idea of what the right process was to pitch a new television show turned out to be a true blessing. If we had known that a pilot episode is usually recorded, budgets are set, and so much more, we would have thought that launching a television program was beyond our reach. In this case, ignorance played to our advantage.

The first thing we did was create a PowerPoint presentation to show our idea to the station where I worked at that time. The answer was immediate. It was a resounding and instant "No!"

Instead of discouraging us, that first refusal spurred us on even more. If they didn't see the value of the project, we would talk to their competitors. But how could we do that without getting into trouble? We decided that the solution was simple: I had to find another job and quit the news station as soon as possible. Four months later, I started teaching as a university professor.

Meanwhile, my husband and I moved forward with the plan, continuously sending emails and banging on doors. Then we received an unexpected email that would get us closer to our dream.

Mr. Barry, one of the city's best-known television managers, was interested in meeting with us. He coordinated the programming of several channels and was curious about our project to create an independent show dedicated to the Latin audience.

I remember Mr. Barry's office very well, because that was the first time I saw something that is present in the offices of programming directors around the world: a wall with dozens of screens designed to monitor the signal of the television station's own channels and those of the competition.

As soon as we started the presentation, I noticed that Mr. Barry paid us a lot of attention. We explained that *SuperLatina* would be a show that would mix entertainment with inspirational stories, that we would take care of the content and editing, and that we needed him to put it on the air on one of his channels.

To this day, I don't know what Mr. Barry saw in us when he decided to give us that first opportunity. All I know is that right there, without even seeing a pilot episode, he said yes.

"I'm going to assign you a cameraman and a director for a couple of hours each week to help you record," said Mr. Barry.

"Perfect. When can we come to the television studio to start recording?" I asked enthusiastically.

"I wanted to talk about that," he said with a serious face. "The station's studios are at full capacity. You can't record the show from here. However, there's another option that I would like you to consider. . . ." Mr. Barry said mysteriously.

From his tone of voice, I knew that the second option was not going to be appealing.

"The owner of the station also owns a shopping center. He is convinced that recording *SuperLatina* from there with a live audience could be an excellent way to increase the number of shoppers visiting the mall."

Without a studio and from a mall? I didn't know anyone who had done a television show in those conditions. Things were starting to get weird, and I had yet to hear the last part.

"There is something else I must tell you. In the building there are no commercial spaces available, so the only alternative I have to offer is to record your show from the mall's carpet warehouse. Would you be willing to accept that possibility?"

Carpet. Warehouse.

I mentally rewound the conversation in the hopes of having misunderstood, but no. Mr. Barry had really said that our "television studio" would be the carpet warehouse in the mall.

"Of course! In one way or another we can make it work. No problem," I hurried to say without much thought as I shook Mr. Barry's hand to seal the deal.

Despite the unusual arrangement, we left the meeting triumphant, because we knew that having a television show, even one that was going to be filmed from a carpet warehouse, was infinitely better than not having one at all. We would have time to figure out how to deal with this unconventional situation.

It's true that the opportunity to do our own show did not arrive traditionally "packaged" . . . but nothing of our immigration story had been predictable either! Perhaps all these crazy circumstances foreshadowed something good.

Andy and I said goodbye to Mr. Barry with seriousness and professionalism, but adrenaline was pumping. As soon as we got to the back of the television station and made sure that no one was watching us, we began jumping for joy like children. Finally, our show would air!

Now that we had gotten the most difficult thing to get—the approval of a television station—all that remained was to buy all the equipment necessary to record and edit the show. We would need microphones, cameras, lights, editing software, and the construction materials for the set.

The good thing was that it was the kind of problem that could be fixed with money. The bad thing was that we didn't have the money to fix the problem. Our savings weren't enough to cover even half of the things we needed to buy in order to launch the show. We urgently needed a bank loan.

Usually, loans under $20,000 are relatively easy to obtain in the United States. However, our case was different: we were immigrants and we did not have enough credit history in the country to get our application easily approved.

We were rejected by all the banks where we applied. To be honest, I think it was a childish mistake to think that getting the money was going to be the easiest part of the equation. The release date of *SuperLatina* was approaching and we still couldn't get the money.

The channel was not aware of any of these difficulties and went ahead with the plans to launch the show, as if nothing was wrong. Meanwhile, Andy and I began to get desperate: four banks had already denied our loan application. If we failed to resolve the situation, we would have no show at all.

I have always been convinced that "God doesn't give you more than you can handle." Every time I feel that things are all over, I check myself, since without fail angels have appeared in my path.

The first angel was an advisor from the Small Business Administration, who suggested that we no longer waste time with the banks and go ask for money directly from local credit unions. The other angel was the employee of the credit union, who trusted the project and approved that glorious first loan even without knowing anything about us. (Andy Espinoza of ASB in Midland, if you read this one day, you should know that I will never forget you!)

Now that the loan had been approved, we began preparing for the premiere. The next challenge was to build the set, which would take several weeks. We bought wooden planks and started trying to find people who could help us with the work. To our amazement, a meteorologist who worked with Andy doubled as carpenter in his spare time to earn extra money. (Yes, you read that right . . . he was a television meteorologist and a carpenter. Reality is stranger than fiction sometimes!)

So we gave the construction work to the carpenter-meteorologist. Every day, after delivering the weather forecast, he would head to the carpet warehouse with his tools to build our stage. Meanwhile, we began to strategize the content of the first programs.

It was so refreshing to create and execute ideas without having to beg for approval from any boss! Did I want to paint my television set hot pink from end to end? I could do it! Did I feel like producing inspirational stories? I could do it! Did I want to request a meeting with a company president to sell advertising? I could do it!

For the first time in my line of work I experienced a sensation that became my drug: total freedom. I worked a lot more hours than when I was part of the news team, and I even had to do physical work. But I had an enthusiasm that did not compare to anything I had experienced before in my life.

I began to feel more in control of my destiny. That feeling of freedom was so beautifully intoxicating that neither the sleepless nights at work nor the economic uncertainties could rob me of it.

On December 1, 2007, my dream of having my own television program came true: *SuperLatina* premiered to a full house in a carpet warehouse in West Texas.

That first episode was dedicated to a charitable cause. We worked with a group of volunteers to complete a surprise room renovation for Yeanna, a local student who was born with cerebral palsy and whose dedication and good humor had won the hearts of everyone in her school. Recording that show in honor of Yeanna is still one of the most rewarding experiences of my career.

If you watch that first episode, you may notice that there are big dark circles under my eyes. The explanation is simple: our budget fell short and we didn't have the money to buy professional lights, so we recorded the first episodes with construction floodlights we bought at Home Depot.

Like usually happens in a premiere, not everything turned out perfectly. Crazy situations were the order of the day, because Mr. Barry had assigned us unintentionally a director who did not speak Spanish, so the poor guy had to guess what I was saying. He switched cameras but had no idea if I were presenting a special report or going to commercial breaks!

That first season was an accelerated course on creativity and innovation. Unexpected situations had to be resolved all the time. And it had to be done quickly and within budget. It was also necessary to adapt to the special circumstances we were dealt.

Since we recorded the show from a carpet warehouse, everything had to be assembled and disassembled every time we recorded. The equipment could not be left in the warehouse from one week to the next, because no one could guarantee that it would not be stolen.

So Andy and I had to get up early every Saturday and perform the following routine: load all the equipment from our apartment to the car; transport it to the carpet warehouse and unload; move and put together the set until it was in the right place; assemble the cameras and tripods; prepare sound mixing equipment, monitors, and other technical stuff; then connect all of that together and plug it in using a series of extension cables taped to the floor.

An hour before filming began, the cameraman and the director arrived to check video and sound. Then we made sure everything was working properly. It was only after doing all that, that I got dressed in my show clothes, began to review my scripts, and did my makeup.

Besides the usual technical complications, doing the show with a live audience from a carpet warehouse in a mall also had other challenges. As the weeks went by, we realized that watching the recording of a television show was not as much fun as it seemed. The shots needed to be repeated several times, which quickly became tedious for the audience. People who came to watch the tapings lost patience and left to continue shopping. From the stage, while hosting the show, I saw the seats empty and my nervousness increased: I knew that if we could not fill those seats in the mall, I could say goodbye to *SuperLatina*.

We didn't know anyone who was doing an independent television show, much less the way we did it. At night, when insomnia took hold of me, I always wondered the same thing:

Are we incredible visionaries or just complete idiots?

One of the problems we faced was that we had two different audiences: we had to offer something compelling for those tuning in from home while keeping the live audience entertained at the mall.

What could we do? We had to improve. After a lot of thought, we came up with a solution as unconventional as our challenge: to ensure our viability in the mall, each episode had to include a segment that was especially attractive to our live audience. We also made sure that this was the last segment we recorded so that the live audience had no choice but to stay until the end.

We tried everything: Zumba segments with sexy girls, magicians, quinceañeras[3] modeling giant dresses. But the two ideas that took the gold in audience retention were exotic pets and kids fashion shows. We became so good at organizing attractive activities for the live audience that we could even predict how many chairs would be filled with family members for each child model we included. Regarding the exotic pets, I humbly believe that part of their success was because I dared to dance with a snake around my neck . . . Britney Spears style!

It's possible that those segments created deliberately to engage the live audience weren't the best that there ever was in the history of world television . . . but at least they were effective and helped us continue learning as independent television producers.

In any case, not every segment of the first season was embarrassing. There were also stories that made me feel proud and that I remember fondly. We had a segment that made dreams come true, and we partnered with local universities in order to surprise students who needed money to continue their education.

With the help of the teachers, we organized "supersecret missions." My favorite part was interrupting classes and surprising students with giant scholarship checks. The generosity of the University of Texas at the Permian Basin allowed us to give away about $100,000 in scholarships.

SuperLatina was beginning to find its way, that's why we were surprised when they called us to an unexpected meeting. There was bad news for us: the millionaire who owned the television station and the mall had changed his mind. The carpet ware-house was going to be remodeled to become a new commercial space.

That meant only one thing for us: only six months after it was born, they canceled *SuperLatina*.

(CONTINUED . . . in the next "In the First Person.")

A Closer Look

Are you curious about the episodes we recorded in the carpet warehouse? We have compiled the worst of the worst for you! Visit www.GabyNatale.com to watch the video.

CHAPTER 6

THE WARRIOR: PERSEVERE FOR YOUR DREAM

Feet, what do I need you for when I have wings to fly?

—FRIDA KAHLO

#VIRTUOUSCIRCLE

THE ONLY FACTOR
THAT CAN PREDICT

A Warrior's

CHANCE OF SUCCESS IS THE
SIZE OF THEIR HOPES.

@GABYNATALE

 Take a photo and share it online using
#VirtuousCircle

The warrior is the fifth archetype of *the Virtuous Circle*. The warrior arrives to teach you that the most epic battle is the one you wage within. Hand in hand with the warrior you will learn to maintain your motivation over time in order to achieve your dream.

The warrior arrives at an opportune time, waking up to accompany you when adversity knocks on your door and you are about to give up. The warrior comes to meet you when you feel disoriented and ready to capitulate because after so many sacrifices, nothing has happened.

With the help of the warrior, you will persevere in what you visualized with the dreamer, planned with the architect, executed with the maker, and perfected with the apprentice.

The warrior is not new in your life. You and the warrior are old acquaintances. It has accompanied you at every crossroads where being strong was your only option.

It's the inner voice that gives you the courage to move forward when you feel the world has turned against you. The warrior is behind an encouraging phrase that comes at the right time, an inexplicable coincidence, or a sense of optimism that invades you without reason at a difficult time. It brings the knowing that greener pastures await you beyond the visible horizon, even if your eyes only see the desert.

The warrior reminds you that what you are looking for is within your reach, but it also warns you that to achieve it you will go through turbulent times that will test you.

The warrior self emerges when the most difficult battles of *the Virtuous Circle* arise. Times you feel you are ready for that big step you've been working hard toward, but no one besides you seems to realize how far you have come. Times when discouragement lurks nearby and will challenge your commitment to your dream.

The warrior manifests in your life with a mission: to teach you that only those who stop fighting are defeated. When uncertainty reigns, the greatest feat is not to climb the highest mountain, nor defeat the toughest adversary. *The most daring and difficult task is to relentlessly overcome the temptation to give up.*

One element alone predicts the chances of warriors' victory. It's not about the power of their attack, the effectiveness of their defense, much less the thickness of their armor. None of these by themselves predict success.

The only factor that can predict how successful warriors will be is the size of their hope.

Those who walk their path armed with extraordinary hope will begin to make decisions based on faith and not on fear; they will have stillness, even if surrounded by turmoil, clarity, though confusion is all around, and peace, even in the midst of turbulence.

Warriors who manage to close their eyes, open their mind, and begin to see beyond the visible will have taken the first step to unleashing unlimited power. They will live according to the maxim that guides the great spiritual gladiators and establishes that *it is possible to win on the outside only those battles that have already been won on the inside. Not the other way around.*

The key to any transcendental change is in battles of the spirit, not in those of humans. Fighting against others is nothing more than an illusion. The real battle is the one fought quietly within our being.

Something to Think About

What spiritual battles would you fight if you knew in advance they were already won?

BATTLES ARE WON INSIDE AND MANIFEST OUTSIDE	
THE INTERNAL BATTLE	IS EXPRESSED EXTERNALLY AS
I DESERVE TO BE LOVED	I ACCEPT / I DO NOT ACCEPT • Being insulted or mistreated by those around me. • Toxic people as company. • Making a priority people who consider me only an option. • Being taken advantage of as long as I am not alone. • Being emotionally manipulated to do what others want me to do.
MY IDEAS AND OPINIONS ARE VALUABLE	I CHOOSE TO / I CHOOSE NOT TO • Share my point of view by participating in work meetings and open discussions. • Express my opinions aloud, even if they are not always the most popular. • Express my disagreement with my partner when I think his or her opinion is wrong.

BATTLES ARE WON INSIDE AND MANIFEST OUTSIDE (continued)	
THE INTERNAL BATTLE	IS EXPRESSED EXTERNALLY AS
I BELIEVE IN MY POTENTIAL	I CHOOSE TO / I CHOOSE NOT TO • Actively seek opportunities in which I can show my talent to the world. • Undertake challenges based on my aptitude and not just my experience. • Press on and try different strategies until the opportunities I seek arise. • Make decisions every day that show my dream is my priority.

WHY IS IT IMPORTANT TO FEED OUR INNER WARRIOR? THE MYTH OF THE LACK OF TALENT

We have all spent time with talented people. You may have had a neighbor with a gifted voice, a relative who was incredibly good with numbers, an especially voluble friend when it came to public speaking, or a schoolmate who was always outstanding in drawing class.

Perhaps you held high expectations for these talented people. If you see them again decades later, however, it's possible you'll be disappointed to learn that many of them no longer practice the skill that made them stand out years ago.

When we meet talented individuals, we anticipate a great future for them, since we tend to assume that talent is rare. That's a mistake. The reality is that talent is extremely abundant. We all have some degree of talent for something.

What is scarce is not talent. *What is scarce is the determination necessary to bring that talent to fruition.*

Every day, skilled athletes who will never play professionally because they don't take their training seriously enough parade through the halls of schools. Around the world, drafts of the next great novel languish on computers and will never see the light of day because their authors failed to finish them. And who knows how many inventions the world is deprived of because their makers don't bother to patent them and make them known. The warrior is the difference between those who stay in the crowd and those who go far.

If you really want to excel, no matter what you do, be committed. Seek excellence, don't just meet expectations. Soon you will notice that you have joined an extremely exclusive club.

None of the trailblazers I have met who have gotten to the top of their profession and developed their talent to the full did it without using focus, determination, and persistence to cultivate their warrior self.

Talent is not a rarity. Perseverance is.

• • •

In This Chapter You Will Find

- The section "The Warrior and Perseverance," where we analyze how to interpret the noes that come your way. Should you keep going or look for new options?
- "Mercenary and Missionary Warriors." Find out why the motivation and "fuel" warriors use on the battlefield is key to predicting their chances of success.
- "Praise of Sadness" (to recover the joy). What to do when the warrior runs out of strength?
- The incredible story of Lizzie Velazquez, a brave warrior who was born with a strong soul in a fragile body.
- The segment "In the First Person," the second part of the story "From the Carpet Warehouse to the Red Carpet."

THE WARRIOR AND PERSEVERANCE:
NO AS PART OF THE PROCESS

During the years I was unemployed (yes, it's *years* with an *s* at the end, because it was more than one) I received hundreds of refusals: by email, by phone, in person during job interviews, and by formal letters declining my scholarship applications.

Some of my major rejections came from big stars as I "guarded" the door of radio and television stations with my resume in hand, hoping to join their team.

At that point, every time a door closed, I took it very personally. It didn't occur to me that the problem might not be me. Perhaps there were budget issues, or they didn't have an open position, or they were looking for someone with other characteristics.

At that time, each *no* was tremendously traumatic. I took it to heart and thought it was irrefutable proof that I had nothing of value to offer the world.

When you take rejection as if you were the victim of a great conspiracy in which everyone hates you and wants to see you lose, you are not doing yourself any favors. On the contrary, you make your life more difficult. In the world we live in, having one or more doors slammed in your face has increasingly become the rule rather than the exception. I hardly know anyone around me who was never fired, never had a project canceled, or never was passed over for a job.

In my case, from the perspective I have gained over the years, it's possible that if any of those emails, phone calls, interviews, or days "guarding" the stations had been successful, my international career and this book would never have existed. It was precisely the succession of refusals I received for years that finally convinced me to consider other options, which opened up new destinations.

How many times had I cried in frustration without imagining that life was doing me a favor by saying no!

If you are willing to become the strong, determined, and courageous warrior that lives in you, you will have to understand that rejection is simply part of the process. And sometimes the negatives that hurt us most contain the most wonderful opportunities.

Not all noes are the same, however. Over the years I have learned that there are two types of noes that come to our road: the "Detour No" and the "Uphill No."

The first type is the Detour No. These are the noes we receive when a situation is so locked up that, no matter how hard or how many times we try, there seems no way to overcome it. The most striking thing about Detour Noes is that they occur even in normally easy-to-solve situations that for some reason get so tangled up that they become extremely difficult to unravel.

When this occurs, we commonly ask ourselves why a usually clear path suddenly fills with obstacles. At that moment, when we are disoriented and looking for an alternative path (detour), chance leads us to a new opportunity.

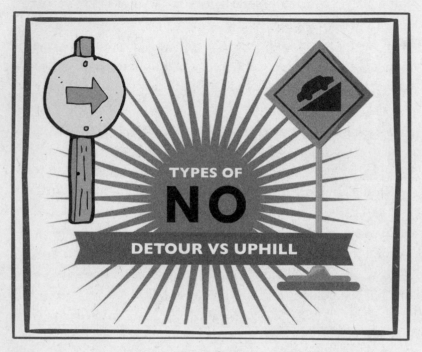

Types of NO.

The Detour No is common currency in matters of the heart: partners who made us feel that the world was ending when they left us unexpectedly also left our heart free to meet a great new love who knows how to make us happy.

The second type is the Uphill No. These are the noes we need to demolish to move toward our next level. They are the ones that require tenacity and insistence in order to leave them behind. It is as if we had a fence we had to jump to move on to the next chapter of our life. In the face of an Uphill No we must persevere with all our strength. These are the noes that any first-time actor must face before having a first opportunity in front of the cameras. The same noes are faced by the executive looking for a position of greater responsibility for which there's lots of competition.

The new possibilities that come into our lives have a very different dynamic according to how they arose. While the opportunities that derive from the Detour No come into our lives *thanks to the fact that we received a no,* the opportunities that come from the Uphill No *come to us despite receiving a no.*

When faced with the first type of no, we need to respond by developing an *open-mindedness* wide enough to consider alternative options. When faced with the second type of no, we need to develop a *laser focus* that allows us to persist until we achieve what we are looking for.

The problem is that when we receive a no, we don't ask ourselves what type of no it is. *Should we persist or look for new options?* At first glance, we have no way of knowing if it will be a "Detour No" or an "Uphill No." Both look the same. Only in retrospect do we realize what kind of no it was.

That's why when receiving a no you must keep a cool head. It's better not to rush to judgement; it may not necessarily be a bad omen for your life. Let yourself be guided by your intuition to see if you can find a clue that will allow you to better interpret the situation.

And before you get discouraged, remember the following:

There are wonderful surprises that come into our lives packaged in the form of a no.

●   ●   ●

Synthesizing . . .

DETOUR NO	UPHILL NO
Result It drives us to new paths.	*Result* It drives us to new levels.
How do the opportunities arrive? Thanks to receiving a no.	*How do the opportunities arrive?* Despite receiving a no.
How to face them? With an open mind.	*How to face them?* With laser focus and persistence.
Some examples of Detour No Those received for working in a profession or industry that is disappearing. Those received as the partner of someone who does not love me or does not respect me.	*Some examples of Uphill No* Those received on our way to higher-ranking professional positions. Those received when taking highly complex exams.

MERCENARY WARRIORS
VERSUS MISSIONARY WARRIORS

A mercenary warrior is one who goes to the battlefield and fights motivated only by economic and personal benefit. Throughout history, the first records of such mercenaries date back to 1,500 BC in Egypt. Documents of the time indicate that Pharaoh Ramses II employed eighteen thousand mercenary warriors, offering them food, water, and the possibility of keeping what they pillaged as payment.

As the centuries passed, the use of mercenary warriors became a common practice. The Greeks, Celts, Romans, and Japanese, among others, used the services of these "soldiers of fortune."

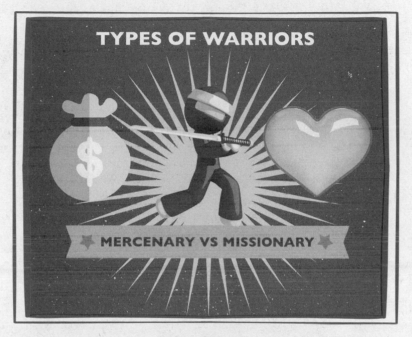

Types of warriors.

The opposite of mercenary warriors were soldiers who represented their nation or fought for an ideal or a mission. They were true heroes willing to give up their lives in defense of their homeland. On the battlefield, these two types of warriors were perceived very differently. While mercenary warriors were despised for their love of money, missionary warriors were admired for their commitment to their ideals.

This differentiation between warriors motivated only by money and warriors inspired by an ideal or mission can be useful outside the military too. In the business world, Randy Komisar, an investor and professor at Stanford University, introduced in his book *The Monk and the Riddle* the distinction between mercenaries and missionaries.

He explains that entrepreneurs who founded their businesses based on a mission—and not only to become millionaires—manage to build more successful and longer-lasting projects and paradoxically end up with more money than those who started their companies motivated only by profit.

According to Komisar, the key to understanding this phenomenon is in the "fuel" each of these groups of entrepreneurs puts into their project. Mercenaries rely on their drive, are opportunistic, and seek short-term results, Missionaries benefit from their passion to propel their business, think strategically, and play for the long term.

This difference in fuel has a fundamental impact on their quality of life. For mercenaries, satisfaction comes only once they can receive the rewards from their project (security, economic well-being, and so on). For the missionaries, on the other hand, well-being derives not only from the material but from the possibilities of working on the project and making an impact on the world through it.

I believe that this distinction can be useful when considering our motivations as we go through *the Virtuous Circle*. For example, it will be much easier to persevere and sustain motivation over time if the warrior has a goal that, in addition to bringing great economic satisfaction, includes a sense of mission.

I am convinced that when your personal goals and interests align with dreams, you become an unstoppable warrior. Those commitments and tasks that mercenaries may perceive as draining personal sacrifices on their road to riches can be experienced as just "part of a fulfilling process" by those warriors who are purpose driven.

Best of all, at the end of the day, it will not only be you who notices the difference. Others will too. *If there's something that shines and doesn't go unnoticed in this world, it's a job done with true love.*

PRACTICAL SUGGESTIONS
TO FEED THE WARRIOR IN YOU

- *The one who chases it, gets it.* Cultivate the warrior's perseverance to minimize the ups and downs of luck. Luck sometimes plays in our favor and sometimes against. You must always do your part so that when the appropriate conditions arise, you can take advantage. Remember that those who persevere constantly will constantly have the chance to succeed. You never know when opportunity will knock on your door.

- *Don't forget that you're passing through.* It's normal that while you persevere toward your dream you have to make decisions that will push you out of your comfort zone. You may have to move out of town, speak in public, change jobs, or make difficult financial decisions. Amid these circumstances, you cannot allow fear or insecurity to paralyze you. When you find yourself at a crossroads and don't know which way to go, take a minute of stillness with yourself and answer this question: *am I making this decision based on fear or faith?*

- *Replace the "why" with "what for."* When something bad happens to us, the first instinct is usually to ask why did this problem occur to *us*. When we ask ourselves that question, we assign ourselves the role of victim and remain powerless. Miracles and tragedies happen every day, why shouldn't something bad come to us too? No one is immune from living with the setbacks of destiny.

But the question that can help you transmute that pain into something positive is "What for?" What lesson can I learn from this episode in my life? Is there anything valuable this experience might teach me? How could this circumstance trigger evolution for me or benefit for others? Sometimes the most valuable growth emerges from the most turbulent moments.

- *Recruit your army.* Your dream doesn't have to be a state secret. Tell others. Share it with the world! Create a routine that allows you to find people to help you with knowledge, time, resources, or contacts. You will need to create the "tribe" that will be your support system.

- *Be strategic with your energy, protect your psyche, and choose your battles wisely.* An easy way is to ask yourself what might be the cause or motivation behind any of your confrontations or conflicts.

  The next time you argue, ask yourself: *Was this an altercation I chose to have or did I just let myself be provoked into it? Did I feel like entering this confrontation or did I just get carried away? Was it worth it?*

  If you are tempted to argue because you are in a bad mood or need to vent and unload on someone, stop. Warriors don't use confrontation to feed their egos or prove their superiority. Confrontation should always be a tool, not an escape valve. Nothing good can come out of an argument started simply to get rid of a bad mood. When in doubt, answer the following questions for yourself: *Am I arguing to come up with a solution or to prove that I am right? Am I saying hurtful things just to relieve my anger and feel better?*

- *Pause yes, resign no.* When you feel you can't do it anymore, give yourself permission to pause. Resting, recharging, and then returning to the ring is a valid option for any warriors who feel like they are on the brink of collapse. Remember that moving slowly is better than not moving forward, and pausing is better than abandoning your path. If you can't continue, take a moment and pause. But never stop! In moments of discouragement or confusion, use your intuition more than ever and keep an eye on the signs of destiny. Then decide your next move.

WHEN THE WARRIOR FEELS DEFEATED: PRAISE OF SADNESS (TO RECOVER THE JOY)

HE WHO HAS A WHY TO LIVE FOR CAN BEAR ALMOST ANY HOW.

—FRIEDRICH NIETZSCHE

Few things can make us feel more dejected than injustice. Sometimes, the person who wins least deserves it. Other times, punishment does not come to those who have done wrong. Occasionally, something horrible and unfair happens to someone with a good heart.

What can we do when cheaters are victorious, when the innocent are punished, or when we face inexplicable misfortune?

Even the most determined warrior stagger in the face of these circumstances. The feeling of helplessness is overwhelming, and it seems as if we are at a dead end.

What happens when something hurts too much? Is it wrong to grieve? Should we move on as if nothing had happened?

Sometimes we feel as if we have to be happy all the time. When something bad happens we say to each other in a well-meaning way: "Cheer up, this too shall pass" or "Put on a brave face." In this way, we seek to encourage ourselves, trying to minimize our pain. We think that a deeply painful circumstance will magically become easier to cope with if we ignore our feelings.

Unconsciously, we label some emotions as good and others as bad. In that dualistic vision of our emotions, being happy is always desirable and feeling sad is always negative, something to be avoided.

But emotions are neither good nor bad. Each one has its function—even those we usually consider less desirable.

For some, having moments of sadness is a sign of weakness.

Nothing could be further from the truth. Sadness is essential for our well-being too. To try to avoid it at all costs is to deny ourselves the possibility of experiencing the full range of human emotions we were created with.

Without sadness, it's impossible to process the profound changes that shake our soul. Sadness often works like the warrior's rest. It's a balm that helps heal deep wounds.

As much as it hurts, we need to go through sorrows in order to feel strong again. To deny ourselves the possibility of being sad is to deny ourselves the possibility of acknowledging that something doesn't make us happy, to deny ourselves the healing process of mourning our losses so we can return to the ring renewed and ready to continue fighting. Tears and laughter are not opposite, but complementary. They are two extremes of the same spectrum. You cannot have one without the other.

Temporarily embracing sadness is not giving up. It's simply allowing ourselves to pause when we can no longer go on.

Sometimes, that pause is just what we need to recharge and return stronger than ever. Remember that to be reborn and recover all its splendor the phoenix needs first to burn to ashes.

It is a mistake to think that sadness is a useless emotion. Sadness helps us accept our losses. It's like a wake-up call when a relationship goes bad; it helps us to reflect on our own mistakes (in order to correct them), and it allows us to empathize with others. How could we be moved by someone else's tears if we couldn't feel sadness in our own soul when we saw others suffering?

Sadness helps us let off steam. Experiencing it makes it possible for us to slowly get rid of the anguish of our soul. Have you noticed that you always feel a little more relieved after crying? Beware of imposing upon yourself a "Dictatorship of Joy." Those who try to force joy on themselves run the risk of numbing their own sensibility and disconnecting from their emotions.

Eating, compulsive shopping, vices, and distractions can become irresistible temptations in our quest to anesthetize ourselves against pain and sadness. But that effort will be in vain. Those shortcuts are nothing more than momentary gratifications that will not solve the underlying problem.

Remember that warriors' strength lies not in winning all the battles but in dusting themselves off and getting back on their feet.

NOTE: Here I want to make a clarification. When I speak of sadness, I am referring to the emotion that is the opposite of joy. In no way am I referring to depression, which is a clinical disease that must be treated by specialists.

•   •   •

Something to Think About

How to use sadness positively?

- *Recognize what relationships sadden you. If you think they are toxic to your spirit, don't hold on to them anymore. As difficult as it may be, let them go. Trust that on the other side of sadness, new companions await you that will replace these tears of sadness with tears of joy.*
- *Promise yourself to become an agent of change in relation to what is causing you distress. Join causes or groups that advocate for a fairer world. That uneasiness you feel today may be the impetus you need to commit even more to your convictions.*
- *If the sadness you feel has been caused by self-destructive behavior, do not wait another minute—seek help. Use the grief you feel today to propel your own personal revolution.*

FROM THE MUD TO THE SPLENDOR: THE LOTUS, A WARRIOR FLOWER

The lotus is an aquatic plant that has been considered sacred throughout history in different religions of ancient Egypt, India, and China. It's a symbol of overcoming, spirituality, and purity.

In addition to its unique beauty, the lotus flower embodies a wonderful metaphor for resilience. It can be said that the lotus is a warrior flower, since its destiny is to emerge victorious from the mud that surrounds it.

The Lotus, a warrior flower.

The lotus flower grows in the darkness of swamps and ponds, surrounded by impurities. As it grows, its stem, which can reach several meters, rises from the pond's bottom to the surface, where it produces a flower of majestic beauty.

Every night, the flower closes and submerges. Each dawn it rises and reopens. During the whole process, the lotus doesn't come into contact with impurities. Its petals remain spotless, unstained by the mud.

The lotus reminds us of the overwhelming force possessed by noble spirits to rise above adversity and overcome it without it corrupting their essence.

• • •

A Voice of Authority

THE WARRIOR—LIZZIE VELASQUEZ

Lizzie Velasquez and Gaby.

"She should do us all a favor and kill herself once and for all!"

"Why did her parents decide to keep her?"

"Light her on fire!"

The comments people left on YouTube were cruel and ruthless. Emboldened by the anonymity of the Internet, users had left pages and pages of insults and cruel jokes addressed to the video's protagonist.

But the worst of all were not the comments but the title chosen by whoever had uploaded the video. "The Ugliest Woman in the World" was the name of the clip that, although it only lasted eight seconds, had already gone viral and had more than four million views.

Meanwhile, a seventeen-year-old girl in Austin, Texas, had taken some time off from doing homework and decided to search for a music video on YouTube to relax. She did not suspect that she was about to live through a moment that would forever alter the course of her life. Due to algorithms and destiny, instead of finding the music clip she was looking for, she came across a very different clip: one that promised to reveal who the ugliest woman on the planet was. When she played it, what she saw made her blood run cold: *she* was the protagonist of the clip!

"After that I spent a lot of nights crying. At first, I thought my life was over. But now I understand that this was when the activist warrior that I am today was born," Lizzie Velasquez explains proudly. She transformed the pain of that day into a mission that has led to her traveling across the planet sharing an antibullying message.

From the beginning, Lizzie's life has not been easy. She was born with a genetic disease called Marfan syndrome that prevents her from gaining weight. When she was born, she weighed only two pounds. She was so tiny that her parents had to buy her clothes at a doll shop.

It was precisely that fragile body, so full of complications, that forged in Lizzie a spirit with the strength of an oak tree. Throughout her life, every stone she has found in her path has become a step on which to climb and move forward with her dreams.

The teenager who was shocked to discover that the Internet had baptized her "the ugliest woman in the world" has

grown into a fulfilled woman who through her message of rad-
ical goodness has become a bestselling author, international speaker, viral YouTuber, and even protagonist of her own
movie.

I visited Lizzie one summer afternoon in her hometown of
Austin. Getting the interview took a year and a half of insistence, but it was worth it. The Lizzie who received me was
celebrating with her mother, Rita. And there was a lot to be
happy about! Against all odds, that girl whose family had been
told by doctors that she would not walk, talk, or see any sem-
blance of a normal life had just become the proud owner of a
beautiful two-story house.

Gaby: You have spoken around the globe. You've been in Ma-
laysia, Mexico, London, Spain, and all across the United States,
just to name a few of the places you have visited. What has
speaking to so many and to such diverse audiences taught you
about our similarities and differences? Do we all worry about
the same things?

Lizzie: Absolutely! The biggest lesson I have learned traveling to all these places is that we do not speak the same languages, but we go through the exact same issues of being insecure and feeling like we're not good enough. And dealing with
being bullied and just wanting to be accepted. And it's funny
because it is the same problem everywhere you go.

Gaby: When I think about your life story . . . from your genetic condition to overcoming bullying to becoming an activist
and traveling around the world to speak to global audiences, I
can't help thinking that the life experience that you have is so
unusual. You may be the only one on the planet who has lived

such a unique combination of experiences. Why do you think it happened to you?

Lizzie: I think this all happened because it was meant to happen. I think this was my life story, and it was a life story that I could never in a million years imagine. And I think I was meant to go through all these obstacles because it made all these accomplishments so much greater.

The talk with Lizzie lasted almost an hour and ended with a hug. I left her home with the certainty of having met a courageous warrior who achieved her own definition of beauty.

A Closer Look

Do you want to know more about Lizzie's story and hear her advice? Visit www.GabyNatale.com to watch Gaby's entire interview with this warrior and discover:

- Which celebrities have become Lizzie's fans and allies in her fight against bullying.
- Lizzie's breaking point in life when she thought about taking her life and how she managed to overcome it.
- Lizzie's advice for everyone who have been a victim of bullying.

•   •   •

In the First Person

From the Carpet Warehouse to the Red Carpet (Part 2)

"The station owner decided to cancel your show. I'm sorry, Gaby," they informed me. I left the meeting stunned. The words echoed in my head, but I still couldn't process them.

Was that really going to be it? So much effort, sweat, and tears just to be on air for six months?

I felt exhausted and had no idea what the next step should be. I had been working for months as a communications professor during the week and as a television producer/host on weekends.

Sometimes I was overcome by despair and thought that everything I had lived had been a great delusion. Perhaps the mistake was not that they had canceled the show but that they had said yes in the first place. For God's sake, it was only three and a half years ago that I had arrived in the United States! Who the hell did I think I was to believe I could have my own television show? Oprah? Ellen?

My phone rang. They told me that in just a couple of weeks we had to vacate the warehouse where we were recording *SuperLatina*. The road ahead seemed so confusing that giving up sometimes seemed a comforting idea.

We had very little time and many decisions to make. Should we continue with the program or should we do something else? What would we do with the set and the stage we had built? Should we keep the cameras and equipment for another time or sell them to begin paying the debts we accumulated to create the show?

And there, in the middle of the disorientation, the warrior in me awoke. Something told me that *SuperLatina* was not done yet. I had no reason to be optimistic about the future, but my inner warrior told me that I should move on anyway. That, despite the turbulent moment, I should learn to look beyond the visible and trust that on the other side of the storm, calm seas awaited me.

We needed to move fast. If the news they had kicked us out spread, it would be even harder to get a new contract with another station. It's the same with television channels as it is with jobs (and with boyfriends!): for some reason, if you already have one, it's easier to get a new one.

Surprisingly, that last-minute move went well. A local channel that knew me for my work on the news agreed to meet with us and made an offer for *SuperLatina* to join its programming. We were relieved. *SuperLatina* would continue on the air, with the novelty that it would be on a station with entirely Spanish-language programming.

This unplanned change had a happy ending, but it left us with a bitter taste: we saw firsthand how volatile the television industry is. Even if you work hard and comply with everything that is required of you, your situation in the industry is precarious: any day the programming strategies can change, the executives who make decisions or even the owners of the station can change, and then—boom!—you're off the air. That is why I'm grateful for every minute that I can work on what makes me happy. I never take any opportunity for granted. I know that in this business, nobody is irreplaceable. Today you are in, tomorrow, who knows.

In the early days of *SuperLatina*, we did something that turned out to be an excellent idea: in 2007 we started uploading our videos to a digital platform that was taking its first steps and seemed promising. It was called . . . YouTube.

I would love to presume that we started uploading *SuperLatina* videos to YouTube because we were great visionaries, supreme communication strategists, and could predict the essential role social networks would play in the future . . . but that would be a big lie!

The real reason we started to share our show on YouTube is simpler: we wanted my mom Cristina, dad Roberto, and mother-in-law Marta, who live in Argentina, to be able to watch the show. This decision, made initially for strictly family reasons, proved to be key later.

Meanwhile, we were still working. We thought that the moments of greatest instability for the show had finally been left behind. *SuperLatina*, which was not even celebrating its first year on the air, had overcome several challenges: the initial financing problems, the logistics of launching from a carpet warehouse, the sudden cancelation of the show, and the relaunching on a different channel. My annual crisis quota was already past full!

I was glad that we had finally achieved some stability after so much uncertainty. It was the first months of 2008, and I naïvely decided to quit my job as a professor.

At that moment, I didn't even imagine how big a misstep I had just taken. Now that we had a television station with programming in Spanish that had promised to give us continuity on screen and local sponsors signing up month to month . . . *what could go wrong?*

What I had not anticipated was that we were in the prelude to what would be the largest economic crisis in the country since the Great Depression.

In the United States, the mortgage crisis began to erupt. On September 15, 2008, the investment bank Lehman Brothers declared bankruptcy. The stock market collapsed, and the financial crisis soon expanded from the United States to the rest of the planet.

Bad news soon arrived for us too. The country was experiencing extreme uncertainty. In a few weeks, economic activity had fallen sharply. No one knew how things would go on, and my clients were no exception. Terrified of what was happening in the world, they sought to lower their costs and cancel advertising spending, including their sponsorships of *SuperLatina*.

One of my main customers at the time, a car dealer who held us in high regard, asked to meet us to break the bad news in person. The worry in the company was that they didn't even know if the brand of vehicles they sold was going to survive the crisis. In that context, what was the point of advertising on television?

I started getting distressed. I no longer had my job as a professor. The show was all I had, and we had money only to cover a few more months. If *SuperLatina* didn't work, I was going to have to go out to look for work again in a recession.

You're a genius, I thought ironically. *You managed to change your country without changing your life: you go from unemployed in Argentina to soon-to-be unemployed in the United States. Ha!*

It was as if history were repeating itself before my eyes. Suddenly, images of the past began to come to my mind: companies going bankrupt, high unemployment rates, people marching through the streets, and the feeling of widespread helplessness . . .

"I have the Midas touch, but vice versa. Instead of transforming what I touch into gold . . . everything I touch becomes trash! Or worse, in recession!" I told Andy as I watched the dire news of what was happening across the country and around the world.

I really couldn't believe what I saw. In the United States, the land of opportunity and abundance, people were losing their homes, their jobs, and even their life savings. It was a tragedy.

"We saw this movie in another country. Just remember what I'm going to telling you: I do not have a crystal ball, but I can tell you exactly what will happen in United States television, because it will be the same as what happened in Argentina in times of crisis," Andy told me firmly. And then he began to enumerate his predictions: budget cuts, mass layoffs, disappearance of shows that required expensive production, freezing of new projects, and things like that.

"I can't believe we have to go through all of this . . . again! After everything we've been through, I feel as if we already have a doctorate in recessions," I complained without thinking much about what I had just said.

Wait. A. Minute.

If we were on the verge of a great recession and we had a "doctorate in recessions," perhaps all was not lost! *What implications could this have? Would it be possible that against all odds we were facing a great opportunity?*

We decided to draw up an emergency plan based on everything we had learned with our doctorate in recessions. For that, we needed to implement changes in three areas: distribution, content, and business model.

The first change was distribution. It was clear we should diversify. We could not continue to have all our eggs in one basket (or on a single television channel in this case). If we wanted to survive, we had to take the show to more cities.

To achieve that, we had to make a second change: content. *SuperLatina* could no longer show only local stories. We needed to create content that would be compelling to all audiences, no matter where they tuned in from.

The third change had to do with the business model. It was obvious that television channels would no longer have the budget for hiring. If they wanted to offer anything new in their programming, they would have to have to join forces with independent producers (like us).

Because we knew that the television stations had empty coffers, we decided to go with a nontraditional proposal: instead of asking them to buy the show from us, we offered to become partners. They would get a show that was ready to air, and in exchange we would get to monetize part of the show's commercial airtime.

As the economic crisis progressed, everything happened exactly how we had anticipated based on our "doctorate in recessions": news and variety programs produced by local channels were being canceled due to lack of resources. Those half hours without programming multiplied throughout the country.

If the entire industry were contracting and we were able to find a formula to expand, perhaps we had a chance for *SuperLatina* to move forward.

Something we never gave up was the intellectual property of the show: *SuperLatina's* rights were never part of the negotiation. They always belonged to us. That way, we could make agreements in different markets without having to consult any of our partners.

Would our survival plan work in the face of the recession? There was only one way to find out. Armed with DVDs and promotional material, we traveled to different cities for months to visit with programming directors.

Since we only had the budget to travel by car, we started with the markets that were closest. That's how I got to know almost every city in Texas and New Mexico. From the El Paso border to the eccentric Roswell (which happens to be the global headquarters of extraterrestrial activity), passing through colonial San Antonio, and opulent Houston.

Convincing programming directors was no easy task. Outside of Midland-Odessa nobody had heard of the show or of us. But little by little our perseverance paid off. By mid-2009, *SuperLatina* was in three cities. Our "doctorate in recessions" was working!

Around that same time, one of our meetings led to a bigger success. In Dallas, a leading station was interested in adding

SuperLatina to its lineup. So much so that we needed to move as soon as possible. Finally, *SuperLatina* would become a regional show. And Dallas, our new home, was among the five most important markets in the country for Latin television!

On the way back to Midland-Odessa, we realized what had happened: the Argentine economic crisis of 2001, one of the most difficult experiences we had lived through, had given us the strength and clarity we needed to take advantage of the opportunity presented to us now.

While we were looking for a house to live in Dallas, we saw the most painful side of the recession in the United States. Many of the properties for sale had been damaged by their own inhabitants.

This phenomenon had spread during the mortgage crisis. Hours before being evicted, occupants, feeling powerless, tried to destroy what until then had been their home. I saw exquisite swimming pools with traces of sledgehammer blows, kitchen walls with hammer holes, and broken windows. It was shocking. Those who think it's impossible to feel the pain of others when entering an empty room should spend a few minutes in one of those houses.

Meanwhile, on the Dallas television channel, plans for *Super-Latina* advanced. After some delays, the station's legal team finalized our contract and all of a sudden we finally had a release date. "Mark your calendars. August 4 is the grand premiere of *SuperLatina* in Dallas!" they informed us.

From that moment, the countdown began. We started working against the clock to get everything ready. We obsessed over August 4, counting the days excitedly.

I am not ashamed to admit that in the weeks leading up to the premiere I became a "timekeeper." A launch requires so much preparation. You have to plan promotional strategies, sales, and produce the content of the show.

(Hurry up. . . . It's almost August 4.)

We also gave the show a new look with more modern graphics and fresh promotional photos. As part of my "timekeeper" style before the debut, we developed all kinds of contingency plans to deal with anything that could go wrong during the recordings.

(Of course. August 4 was just around the corner!)

There were special instructions in case a guest failed to show up, in case there was a last-minute technical problem, in case we wanted to record outdoors and there was bad weather. We thought we had everything covered, but how wrong we were. (As they say, if you want to make God laugh, you just have to tell Him your plans.)

What we had not contemplated was that no matter how much you try to control everything, sometimes life gets in the way. And that was exactly what happened: a few days before the regional premiere, I received unexpected news.

"The diagnosis is bad, Gaby. They found a carcinoma," my mother told me on the phone. I listened attentively, keeping calm while she explained some medical details I didn't quite understand.

When I hung up the phone, I went on Google to investigate. Reading the definition of carcinoma was like getting punched in the stomach: A carcinoma is a form of malignant cancer. Carcinomas are the most common type of cancer.

I called my mother again to confirm the news. We were both so shocked that we almost didn't dare to say that dreaded word.

"Mom, I didn't understand . . . carcinoma," I said in a small voice. "Do you have cancer?"

"Yes, my dear daughter."

The silence seemed like an eternity. And we let each other cry on the phone. My mom had breast cancer and needed to start treatment as soon as possible.

"And what will happen now? What are the next steps?"

"The doctors already gave me a date for my operation. It will be August 4."

August 4.

The date we had been waiting for the last couple of months now took on another meaning. Of all the days of the year and of all the years I have lived, what were the chances that two such important events—my mom's operation and the show's launch in Dallas—would occur on the same day?

I decided to take this as a sign that would give me courage in a difficult time. For some while, when things like this happened to me, I would take them as happening for a reason and not as mere coincidences. Besides, I always told my audience and the interviewees that they should remain hopeful. This time, it was my turn to lead by example.

When the long-awaited August 4 finally arrived, it found me surrounded by makeup, hairspray, and curlers. Not because I was preparing to go on the air, however, but for another reason.

I was in Argentina to accompany my mother for her operation. To keep us entertained, I had told her that we were going to do a "glam session" of hairstyling and makeup. The idea was to get to the presurgical exams made up like a queen.

The "glam session" was our feminine and somewhat crazy way of looking for an excuse to smile on a sad day. The only condition I set as an improvised makeup artist and hairstylist was for my mom not to look in the mirror until I finished so that she could enjoy a "surprise makeover."

And oh man, did she have it! Seeing the final result (which included beautiful golden glitter) my mother claimed that I had gone too far and made her up like a cabaret singer. The point is that it had gotten late, and we no longer had time to adjust the makeup to her liking, so laughingly she told me how she was leaving a "golden glitter trail" on each checkup machine.

Luckily, my mom's operation was a success. I was able to return more composed to Dallas, where the show had continued its normal schedule after airing episodes I had recorded before flying to Argentina.

The following years we focused on reinvesting, improving the quality of the show, and traveling to get the best stories we could. Little by little, the fruits of our labor began to arrive: we opened AGANARmedia (our own marketing agency for Latino audiences), more clients joined, and awards nominations came in.

Also, our YouTube channel began to take on a life of its own. The gabinatale channel that we had opened in 2007 so that family who lived far away could see the show had multiplied in views (today it exceeds 45 million) and became a fundamental tool when it came to expanding the show.

In 2014, seven years after that ragged start from a carpet warehouse in Odessa, we received the call we had dreamed of since our first episode: a national channel offered to air *SuperLatina* from coast to coast in the United States.

(CONTINUED . . . in the next "In the First Person").

CHAPTER 7

THE CHAMPION: ACHIEVE YOUR DREAM

Not even a god could change into defeat
the victory of a man who has vanquished himself.

— GAUTAMA BUDDHA

#VIRTUOUSCIRCLE

BEING AS WE
TRULY ARE
MAKES US
Champions.

@GABYNATALE

T he champion is the sixth archetype of *the Virtuous Circle*. This is the stage of the harvest: your dream will finally come true. So get ready for glory.

The times of the champion are perfect. They come to your life not when you want, but when you are ready to receive them. Not a day before. Not a day later. Try as you might, there is no way to force their arrival.

For the champion to appear in your path, three elements must be aligned: preparation, desire, and opportunity.

All three elements must be present *simultaneously*. If you have preparation and opportunity but no desire, you will lack the necessary determination to fight for your dream. If you have the desire and opportunity but no preparation, you will lack the knowledge necessary to bring your dream to fruition. If you have the desire and preparation but no opportunity, you will lack that stroke of fate to achieve your dream. Only through the combination of the three elements can you invoke the champion so that it appears in your life and you can fulfill your dream.

With the help of the champion you will achieve what you visualized with the dreamer, planned with the architect, executed with the maker, perfected with the apprentice, and fought for with the warrior.

Wise champions choose prudence. They know that the pride of a success only lasts, at most, until the next failure crosses their path. They have learned that victory and defeat are not final destinations but transient states. That's why they don't lose humility in times of triumph nor hope in times of disappointment. The path has taught them that success and failure are two sides of the same coin.

The champion defies logic. It surprises us. It's unpredictable. The champion is the inexplicable force that turns defeat into victory at the last instant. Or the unexpected virtuosity of a rookie who manages to land a blow that takes an opponent out of the battle. The champion is the sacred fire that rewards the hearts of the rebels who believe in their greatness and launch themselves into the conquest of the unknown.

Those who cultivate the champion within, cultivate faith in their own greatness. And they discover, blow by blow, a secret that only the wise know: *on the other side of the ring there were never other contestants, only their own fears.*

CLARIFICATION:
In the world of sports, we call "champion" the contestant who defeats one or more opponents and takes the top prize. That is to say, someone must always lose so that another has the chance to win. The champion in *the Virtuous Circle* is understood in a broader sense, in which an achievement doesn't have to be preceded by someone else's defeat. At the end of the day, the greatest victories are those we achieve over ourselves.

In This Chapter You Will Find

- "The Five Deadly Sins That Surround the Champion."
- The section "In the First Person," with the third part of the story "From the Carpet Warehouse to the Red Carpet."
- "A Voice of Authority" interview with Mexican actor Eugenio Derbez, who shares with Gaby his "champion" moment when he broke Hollywood box office records with his debut as movie director.

THE FIVE DEADLY SINS
THAT SURROUND THE CHAMPION

The sixth archetype of *the Virtuous Circle*, the champion, marks the accomplishment of the dream for which you worked so hard. It's a moment of celebration but also a time to reflect on the road traveled.

Usually it is said that it is in times of failure, not success, when we learn the most. But the champion's passage through our lives also contains valuable lessons. As you move forward in the direction of your successes, you are likely to find resolution to some of the doubts that haunted you in the past. At the same time, new questions arise.

Therefore, in this chapter, you will find some challenges that come up when you have achieved the dream or goal you initially set for yourself. I call these challenges the "capital sins" of the champion, and the most common are the following five:

1. FRIVOLITY: Champion, DO NOT confuse the lasting with the ephemeral.

2. GUILT: Champion, you DO NOT have to "pay" with pain for your success.

3. PRIDE: Champion, DO NOT confuse what is yours with what is borrowed.

4. LAZINESS (INTELLECTUAL): Champion, DO NOT rest on your laurels.

5. SHAME: Champion, DO NOT forget where you come from.

CAPITAL SIN #1: FRIVOLITY
Champion, DO NOT confuse the lasting with the ephemeral.

If your dream is based on connections, beauty, or youth, you will soon realize that you are sitting in a house of cards. At the slightest breath of wind, everything will collapse.

Anything you build on a weak foundation is bound to collapse sooner or later. This seems obvious, but too many people forget it when it comes to their projects.

I work in an industry (the media business) where it's increasingly common to find people who prioritize packaging over the content. They build careers that often have a meteoric rise, but a steep fall when their time has passed. In your life you will also come across these "champions with feet of clay" who sadly become disposable when the package fades or when their benefactor stops protecting them.

Your dreams are not a race. If you want your projects to last over time, whatever you do, always bet on substance. Only those who plan their professional future by building on ideas survive the test of time.

You don't need to work in front of the cameras to feel pressure to keep up with appearances of image or class. Social media is filled with images that portray perfect lives that do not exist. That is why you need to cultivate the clarity that will allow you to separate the noise from the real.

Pepe Mujica, the former president of Uruguay whose austere lifestyle even as president created a cult, left many thinking with this reflection about frivolity and consumption, which went viral on social media:

We invented a mountain of superfluous consumption, and you have to throw everything away and live shopping and dumping. And what we are spending is our life, because when I buy something, or you buy something, you do not buy it with money, you buy it with the time of your life you had to spend to get that money. But with this difference: the only thing that cannot be bought is life. Life is spent. And it is miserable to spend life to lose freedom.

In a world so desperate to impress others, the greatest act of rebellion is perhaps to live your life in an authentic way, focusing on the substance and not the shell.

CAPITAL SIN #2: GUILT

Champion, you do NOT have to "pay" in pain for your success.

The first time I realized I felt guilty because I had succeeded in something I was sixteen. I had managed to pass the entrance exam for one of the most demanding universities in my country, and I felt very proud of myself. Passing that exam had required a lot of dedication on my part, including traveling regularly to another city to take extra classes for months in my last year of high school.

Upon hearing the news of my admission, the first thing I did was something that seems unusual to me today: I went to my room, gathered my entire doll collection, and took them to an orphanage as a gift. Undoubtedly it was a nice gesture, but behind that action was something more than kindness or charity. I was convinced that if something good happened in my life, I had to balance it in some way: for every gain there must be a loss.

At that time, I was too young to realize what was happening to me. My dad, who had witnessed the scene, wrote me a very loving letter, which he titled "Dolls Don't Pay." It explained to me that while helping others is always praiseworthy, thinking that I had to part with my dolls for having passed the exam was a mistake. I could have my good news and my dolls. And there was nothing wrong if I wanted to.

In his note, my dad explained to me that life is not governed by a law of compensation for joys, where every laugh should be paid with a tear. And if I didn't pay attention, I was going to grow up going on a guilt trip every time I achieved something. That letter marked the first time I started thinking about guilt. I realized how common it is to feel it, especially at times where things are going well.

Guilt can be expressed in many ways: sabotaging your own efforts, dimming your light so that others around you feel more comfortable, letting people around you take advantage of you because "overall, you have done well and they have not done as well," or feeling that you are an imposter when the reality is that you have earned every achievement.

Pay attention the next time something good happens to you and see if you are unconsciously thinking that something bad is on its way. Remember that, as my father says, "Dolls Don't Pay."

CAPITAL SIN #3: PRIDE
Champion, DO NOT confuse what is yours with what is borrowed.

In the movie *The Informant*, Al Pacino plays Lowell Bergman, a star producer of *60 Minutes*. Based on real events, the film relates the exhaustive investigation that revealed how tobacco industry abuses were jeopardizing the health of the population.

The Al Pacino character leads the research team and has secured a series of phenomenal exclusives for the show. In the middle of the film, things get complicated and this star producer has a moment of crisis. He needs to know how much of his success is his own doing and how much came from belonging to the team of one of the most watched programs in the country.

"I am Lowell Bergman from *60 Minutes*," he explains vehemently. "You know, if you take *60 Minutes* away from that phrase, nobody calls you back." When I saw this part I had to pause! There was a lot to think about.

In a world where egos grow so easily, Lowell's self-examination becomes more useful than ever. What part of your success is based on your own merits and what part on the place you occupy? What opportunities that you enjoy today depend on your position in your company, and which ones would still be there if you lost your job? How many of those around you today would still be by your side if your job vanished?

I have seen firsthand with great sorrow how doors were closed to high-level executives, talented journalists, and television stars when they lost their jobs. How different their luck would have been if they had been as insightful as Al Pacino's character before it was too late! How much lighter they would have felt without all that arrogance weighing them down!

Dear champion, do not fall into the trap of thinking that you are someone very important because of the work you do. The more inflated the ego, the harder the blow when something does not go as planned. I have seen "chiefs of chiefs" sitting on pumpkins—like Cinderella after midnight—when they were fired, and in the blink of an eye the champion's flatterers, invitations to VIP events, and the attention of colleagues disappeared.

Beware of the temptation to believe yourself superior to others. Keep your eyes wide open and do not confuse what is yours with what is borrowed. Do not get giddy over your degree, the size of your office, or your company's prestige. All these things can be comforting, and it is good that you enjoy them, but never forget that they are passing through. No one is irreplaceable.

The opposite is also true: when things go wrong, don't think that a dismissal or lack of opportunities reflects your value as a person or professional. Remember that while a great job doesn't make you superior, losing that position doesn't make you inferior.

Be smart and take advantage of your time in each job. Perfect and cultivate the talents, relationships, and opportunities that may be useful to no matter who employs you or what your tasks.

There is absolutely nothing wrong with working for someone else . . . as long as you don't forget that at the end of the day, you must first work for yourself.

CAPITAL SIN #4: LAZINESS (INTELLECTUAL)
Champion, DO NOT rest on your laurels.

**THE ILLITERATE OF THE TWENTY-FIRST CENTURY
WILL NOT BE THOSE WHO CANNOT READ
AND WRITE, BUT THOSE WHO CANNOT
LEARN, UNLEARN, AND RELEARN.**

—ALVIN TOFFLER

Images of the Facebook headquarters. When Mark Zuckerberg, Facebook's
founder, arrives at his office, the sign that greets him bears his company's name
(top left). Upon returning home, the sign that says goodbye bears the name
of the company that previously occupied that space (bottom left).
A good reminder that everything is transitory.

Some champions become lazy once they get what they are
looking for. They lose curiosity and fall into routines. As time
passes, they offer old answers to new questions, and they end up
quashing their own success.

I learned one of the most shocking stories of "extinct champions" a few months ago, when I had to deliver a keynote speech
during a business conference at Facebook headquarters in *Silicon
Valley* as part of the Summit of the Americas. During my visit, I
took the opportunity to tour the famous headquarters of the largest social network on the planet.

What struck me most about the campus is the story behind the sign at the entrances. When passing through the front, you see a sign with the legendary "Like" icon that is synonymous with Facebook around the world. On the back of the sign, however, you see something different. And that is the most interesting part of the story.

In 2011, when Facebook needed new offices, its founder, Mark Zuckerberg, decided to buy the property that today is occupied by the Facebook campus from a company called Sun Microsystems.

Sun Microsystems was a company that manufactured expensive servers and was an industry leader in the 1990s. Years later, as consumers massively adopted desktop PCs, Sun Microsystem's powerful servers began to be increasingly obsolete. Like Blockbuster, Sun Microsystems could not adapt to changes in the industry and disappeared.

When buying the property, Zuckerberg decided to make a very particular decision: instead of replacing the entrance sign with a new one, he simply turned the existing one around and hung the Facebook sign on the front of the old sign.

The reason was simple and powerful. He decided to keep the deteriorating Sun Microsystems sign as a daily reminder of what can happen when we fail to adapt to new times.

Every morning when he arrives at his office, Zuckerberg sees the sign on the front with the symbol from the company he founded while still a student and that became a global phenomenon. But when he goes home, it is Sun Microsystem's, not Facebook's, sign he sees last. This is a warning of the dangers of resting on your laurels: what is a success today, tomorrow may only be a memory.

Making changes is scary sometimes. But what happens when we refuse to make them is usually even more frightening.

CAPITAL SIN #5: SHAME
Champion, DO NOT forget where you come from.

There is a special race of champions who, with each step along their path to success, forget who they were and where they came from. They are the champions who suffer from the "amnesia of success."

As they rise, they begin to put so much focus on pleasing new friends and acquaintances that they go to the extent of erasing their roots, personal opinions, and sometimes even their true name in their attempt to win other people's approval. They fear their new circles will reject them if they show themselves as they are.

As their horizons expand, so expands the shame they feel for their roots. That's why it's common for them to become chameleons, creating fictional stories and personalities they hope will fit better into their new "habitat."

What these "amnesic champions" fail to realize is that, in their attempt to satisfy other people's expectations, they are obscuring their greatest treasure: their identity.

That personal story, those "defects" or imperfections, is no cause for shame. They are the raw material of our being and what makes us unique.

KINTSUGI: The Japanese Art of Loving Scars
Kintsugi 金継ぎ is an ancient Japanese ceramic technique that consists of repairing objects by joining their broken parts with gold threads. Instead of trying to hide imperfections, *kintsugi* uses them as a starting point to recompose and give character to the object.

For those who practice *kintsugi*, the cracks and wounds left by time are not something to be hidden but rather a source of pride. It's precisely the breaks, not the flawless smooth surfaces, that tell the story of the object and give it its unique character.

Kintsugi contains a poetic and powerful idea: it's our scars that make us beautiful and give us the chance to be reborn.

Kintsugi.

A Voice of Authority

THE CHAMPION—EUGENIO DERBEZ

When *Instructions Not Included* became a blockbuster, it took everyone by surprise. Even established directors and producers in Los Angeles had never heard of the film created by comedian Eugenio Derbez, who had beaten the Hollywood heavyweights at the box office.

Gaby is pictured with the tireless actor, host, and Mexican producer
Eugenio Derbez. We took this photo a few hours before the
premiere of *Instructions Not Included*, the film that would
establish him as the most promising Latin star in Hollywood.

*"How was it possible that a 'total stranger' had managed
to create such an overwhelming instant success?"* studio executives asked themselves when they first saw the photo of
Eugenio Derbez in the Los Angeles newspapers.

What executives did not know was that this "instant success" in the United States had had a forty-year career, and
that the movie that came "out of nowhere" to break box office
records had been twelve years in the making. During that time,
Derbez was in charge of not only writing the script but also

producing it, starring in it, directing it, and even taking the lead in the editing process.

When I met with Eugenio to interview him, it was only a few hours before the premiere that would change his life forever and make him the champion of the box office.

We met in Texas, during one of the last stops before the premiere, to talk about this bittersweet story he had created about the bond between a single Mexican father and his American daughter. Derbez had the typical nervousness that precedes the launch of a new project, but he also felt the relief of being at the end of several intense weeks of promotion.

First he told me about the years of preparation he had to go through to create the film. One of the most formative experiences in making the leap to Hollywood had been his time on the stages of Broadway.

"I had to face many of my fears. The biggest one was the language. For me, English has been a very big barrier. The biggest challenge was to encourage myself to work on Broadway. I had to do four monologues in English, and I was extremely nervous. Before going onstage, I was shaking and sweating," he explained with passion.

In addition to language, there were other challenges he had to face to find new horizons. To take advantage of his first opportunities in the United States, Eugenio had to organize an unconventional work schedule: every weekend he traveled back and forth between Mexico City and New York. He did so in conditions that very few established stars of Latin television would have accepted.

"I was not paid a salary here in the United States. Much less given money to cover the costs of hotels or air tickets. It was something I would invest in as long as they let me step on a Broadway stage. I did it for two and a half years before I finally was able to earn my space," he confessed with a tone of complicity, like someone telling you about a prank.

For Derbez, his forays into Broadway and his movie *Instructions Not Included* represented not only the opening of new horizons. They were also, above all, a quintessential victory over the prejudices of the movie industry.

The seed that grew into *Instructions Not Included* was not in the money that financed the movie, nor in the film's detailed scripts, nor in any visionary marketing plan. The seed of the film that would change Derbez's life forever lay in the pain of one who felt unfairly excluded.

Few know this, but the creator of *Instructions Not Included* knows all too well the bitter taste of rejection. For years, he knocked on the doors of the most renowned Mexican directors in the hope that they would give him a chance to work in film. But the effort was in vain. "You're too commercial," they would tell him over and over again when he was rejected for projects. Crazy as it seemed, his great popularity on television was a handicap when it came to making the transition to the big screen.

Fed up with being pigeonholed and having the door slammed in his face, Derbez decided to create his own opportunities. He turned frustration into desire.

Finally, after more than a decade of effort, *Instructions Not Included* was released on Labor Day weekend in 2013. The little low-budget film directed by the comedian nobody would hire for the big screen grossed more than $100 million. It was so successful that it became the most watched Spanish-language film in U.S. history and the highest-grossing Mexican film of all time.

The same weekend of the movie's premiere, Eugenio Derbez turned fifty-two. His birthday present was to prove that there is no dream too big when the desire, preparation, and opportunity align for you to become the champion.

In the First Person

From the Carpet Warehouse to the Red Carpet (Part 3)

On the red carpet of the Emmy awards, hours before the academy announced that, for the first time in its history, an independent show in Spanish would receive two statuettes on the same day. It was my show, *SuperLatina*.

"The champion doesn't arrive when you want but when you are ready. The champion's advent cannot be rushed or delayed." For a person who is such a control freak as myself, this was one of the most difficult lessons to learn.

There is a long list of things that I have aspired to through the years—like my first job as a journalist, my moves from place to place, or my show—that did not happen as quickly as I would have liked. Many times, the wait seemed endless. I felt that the champion was coming to my life . . . but in slow motion!

Over the years, I discovered that wanting to control everything was not only exhausting but also unproductive. I learned that the best way to use my energy was to focus on what did depend on me: preparation and desire (the first two elements of the champion). In this way, I made sure that when the opportunity arose (the third element of the champion and the one we can least control) I would be as ready as possible to seize it.

That change of approach brought me very pleasant surprises. I discovered that, while it was not possible to rush the champion, there was no way to stop him either. When the champion's time has come, the unlimited power of dreams works wonders even on things that at first glance seem almost unattainable.

The story I will tell you below is a testament to this.

✕

When I opened my email inbox, my jaw dropped: "Congratulations, you are nominated for the Daytime Emmys!" I read and reread the email without being able to believe the news. The sender was none other than the National Academy of Television Arts and Sciences of the United States. It announced that *SuperLatina* had not one but two nominations! We would compete in the categories "Outstanding Daytime Talent in a Spanish

Language Program" and "Outstanding Entertainment Program in Spanish." The awards show would be in just weeks and would take place in the largest hotel in Los Angeles.

I didn't need to be told anything about this awards ceremony. I knew by heart what the ceremony was about from watching it on television. On that stage they had awarded legends that have been great role models for me like Oprah Winfrey, Barbara Walters, and Ellen DeGeneres.

To say the nominations were a surprise for us would be a huge understatement. In fact, when Andy arrived at the office and I shared with him the big news, he didn't believe it. I had to show him the email on the computer screen because he thought I was joking.

"And who are we competing against?" he asked curiously, now that he realized that this was serious.

I was so shocked by the news I hadn't even checked all the details about our category. So I entered the E! Entertainment website and carefully reviewed the list of nominees. There I finally saw the other contestants.

"Mmm . . . We are up against CNN and Univision. We are the only independent show." I replied as I read the details.

"Oh, then there is no need to worry," Andy said wryly. We are competing *only* with the largest news network on the planet and the most watched Latin channel in the United States.

We burst into laughter. Without a sense of humor it would have been impossible to survive the ups and downs we went through with the show all these years. And to tell you the truth, Andy was right: *There was no reason to worry*. We had already done everything that was within our reach by preparing the best content we could. The rest of the process was no longer up to us.

How liberating to feel that the end result was not in our hands! Actually, the chances that an independent program could beat communication titans like CNN and Univision in the Emmys were so remote that we honestly didn't feel the slightest pressure to win. So we decided to devote ourselves to deeply enjoying the moment beyond whatever happened on the day of the awards.

The first thing we did was give thanks. We called family, colleagues, friends, and sponsors to express our appreciation. We were especially pleased to give the news to our team at the channel (VmeTV), who believed in us enough to put the show on the air nationwide.

Upon hearing the good news, Doris Vogelmann, our programming director, told me something I will never forget: "Not everything is money, Gaby. Sometimes, having a large budget does not guarantee anything. Magic cannot be bought."

The unlimited power that is unleashed when we put our energy and our dreams into action never ceases to amaze me. Just a little while back I had been one of the people stuck to the screen watching the awards in pajamas from home . . . and now I would have the opportunity to be part of the most important award show in the industry!

As the date of the Daytime Emmys awards approached, I began to feel butterflies in my stomach. The academy team was in constant communication with us to coordinate all the details they needed from *SuperLatina*, ranging from videos to the name of the designated person who would take the stage if we won.

"Do you have a thank-you speech prepared in case we win?" Andy asked when the ceremony was only a few weeks away.

The truth is that I had not wanted to prepare anything because I didn't want to jinx It. I had been nominated for other awards before, not once or twice . . . but seven times! And I didn't get lucky in any of them.

Anyway, when we were just a few days from the Emmys, I decided to prepare a speech just in case. Given the remote possibility that we would win, I did not want to become one of those winners who after waiting a lifetime for that moment, finally take the stage to accept the award only to make a fool of themselves because they don't know what to say.

We arrived in Los Angeles the day before the ceremony so we would be well rested. We wanted to enjoy the whole experience without running around. Not many people know this, but the activities for nominees begin days before the ceremony. One of them is the gifting suite, which is a kind of private exhibition offered by the event's sponsors to entertain the nominees.

The morning of the awards day flew by. At about ten o'clock, the beauty squad arrived to help me get ready for the big red carpet. The process of styling, makeup, and changing clothes lasted about three hours. As soon as we finished, it was time to go to the event. Andy was already bathed, combed, perfumed, and ready with his tuxedo. It had taken only twenty minutes, and he looked gorgeous.

Before leaving the room, we kissed and took a deep breath. We had worked for almost ten years to have the opportunity to be part of a ceremony like the one we were about to experience that night. Whatever happened, we already felt like winners.

We went through the security checks and arrived in the red-carpet area. Behind the scenes, the organizers received all the nominees, presenters, and the invited stars to coordinate their entrance on the red carpet. The place was full of familiar faces: the cream of the crop of U. S. television. The hosts of the most important talk shows, soap opera actors, and many of the celebrities I always see in magazines were waiting for their turn to walk on the carpet. Before entering the carpet, I even had the pleasure of taking a picture with Elmo, my favorite *Sesame Street* star!

Walking the carpet of an event like the Emmys is quite an experience. Wherever you look there are flashes and cameras.

Everything is hurried, frenzied, and it happens in the middle of a lot of screaming. As soon as we finished taking photos and being interviewed by the media, I took a break and decided to make a video for *SuperLatina* fans. I wanted to share the moment with them. At the end of the day, it was their support that had allowed me the privilege of being there.

When I put the phone down, I found myself right next to a familiar face. Extremely familiar. It was Larry King. The most emblematic interviewer in the history of CNN was standing in front of me. King was nominated in two categories and had brought his wife and his whole family to accompany him on this great day. For someone like me who is dedicated to producing talk shows, it was a great honor to meet him on the red carpet.

As we went inside, the Daytime Emmys production team welcomed us and indicated which table we would be sitting at. It was a huge and majestic hall. At the front was a spectacular stage with giant screens, guarded at both ends by oversized Emmy statuettes several meters tall.

One of the first things we noticed upon arriving at our table was that we had been lucky with the location. We were near the stage, so we were going to be able to appreciate the show in all its glory.

On each plate rested a booklet with the event's program. We discovered that our two categories were among the first ten they would announce that night. For better or worse, we would soon find out about our fate.

I sent a message through social networks to share with our followers, family, and friends that we were already at the ceremony, ready to enjoy the show. I received nonstop messages from well-wishers. Suddenly, the lights went out and they asked for silence.

The show was starting!

Mario López, the host of *Access Hollywood*, welcomed us from the stage. I was relaxed and enjoying the opening number when I felt someone touching my back. When I turned around I saw a woman squatting with headphones and a walkie-talkie in the dark. It was one of the producers.

"Please, don't let the *SuperLatina* team get up from the table or go to the bathroom now. There're only a few minutes left before the category 'Outstanding Entertainment Program in Spanish' in which you are competing. We need all the nominees to remain in their seats," she said in whispers.

I assured her that we would. At that moment, my serenity went out the window and I could no longer pay attention to the show. Andy and I began exchanging nervous glances as we tried to interpret the movements we saw around us. The reality is that we had never seriously considered the possibility that we would win. What if today was the day David beat Goliath?

"Gaby, there's only a couple of minutes left for our category. Do you want to practice the speech just in case?" Andy offered me lovingly.

As always, I had written my speech on a piece of paper, but I hadn't taken it out of my purse. I unrolled the paper and tried to start repeating it in a low voice. Meanwhile, onstage the characters from *Sesame Street* and Mario Lopez kept talking, but my brain had already shut them out.

"These hands that hold an Emmy today . . . These hands that hold an Emmy today . . ."

Just saying the initial sentence made my voice break, and I couldn't continue. It was a totally absurd situation.

I hadn't won any Emmy and I was already crying at the table!

The television network executives who shared the table with us looked sideways at the little scene not understanding a thing.

"Gaby, please focus. The speech you prepared is very nice, but if you start crying at the first sentence, you won't be able to say anything," Andy said firmly, looking me in the eye.

"These hands that hold an Emmy today are the same hands . . . they are the same hands . . ."

I kept trying to say the words, but I felt a lump in my throat of nervousness and emotion that didn't let me speak. Suddenly, I felt a powerful light that dazzled my face. A cameraman standing beside our table pointed at us with his lens.

What does it mean that this guy is pointing at us with the camera like this? Do they want to capture the image of the "good losers" applauding graciously? Or maybe it's something else?

The time had come. On the stage they announced the nominees of our category. While the videos were running, shouts and applause encouraged each of the candidates. Andy and I held hands tightly.

Then, from the stage, the host said the same famous phrase I had heard so many times while watching awards ceremonies in my pajamas from home:

"And the winner is . . . "—there was a silence that seemed to last forever—"*SuperLatina* with Gaby Natale!"

In a second, all the challenges I had lived through crossed my mind: the sacrifices my parents made to give me a good education, my unemployment just after I graduated from university, the loneliness of the early days as an immigrant in an unknown land, the uncertainty of the citizenship process, the sleepless nights editing stories when we had just launched the show, and the hundreds of meetings trying to convince executives for ten years that an independent show was worth it.

No, I didn't need a piece of paper to read the speech. I knew very well what I felt. So I went onstage and opened my heart:

These hands that are holding a Daytime Emmy award today are the same hands that ten years ago were holding a brush and a paint can to paint the first set of our *SuperLatina* show.

Together with Andy Suárez, my life and business partner, we decided to create *SuperLatina* from a carpet warehouse in Odessa, Texas, just motivated by the idea of producing television that inspired us.

This award is dedicated to dreamers, to rebels, to those who wake up every day and don't allow anyone to define their capabilities. Never think that you are too old, fat, ugly, gay . . . or too undocumented to make your dream come true.

I wanted to dedicate my speech to the transformative power of hope put into action. Because what seemed impossible—that a small television show born in a carpet warehouse took the trophy home—had come true.

When I finished thank-yous, they took us backstage. The whole situation was as if we were inside a movie. The producers guided us to the press rooms, where entertainment reporters were waiting to interview us and take photos. After the interviews and pictures in the first three press rooms, I saw from the corner of the eye that they were beckoning us. An agitated producer had arrived in the press room.

"You are Gaby Natale. You have to go back to the ceremony area right now! In a minute the other category you are nominated for is being announced," he said in a tone that seemed to be one step away from having a heart attack.

The producer, Andy, and I literally ran out of the press room. It seemed like I was in a marathon, but in heels with an Emmy in hand. Between strides Andy and I looked at each other, not understanding anything that was happening.

We arrived breathlessly backstage just for the moment when the videos of the nominees were showing on the giant screen. Thirty seconds more and it would have been too late!

"And the Emmy winner for Best Talent in a Spanish-Language Program is . . . ," said the host, "Gaby Natale!"

An Emmy for the best television host in Spanish-language television! The dreams, the preparation, the desire, and the opportunity had lined up!

I went up to the stage trying to catch my breath, stunned and unable to believe what was happening. I gave impromptu thanks to everyone (I didn't have a second speech ready!) and went backstage trying to assimilate all the emotions I had experienced that night.

Days later, I learned something that filled me with pride. *Super-Latina* had made history: it was the first time an independent show in Spanish won at the Daytime Emmys. It made me happy to think that this unprecedented recognition could encourage other people to believe in their own dreams.

Through all my years in my career I had been told more than once that to succeed I needed to be different. That in order to gain my space in the industry I needed to change my style, weight, appearance . . . even my accent!

I never listened to them.

On the big night of the Emmy awards I confirmed what I have always known: *staying true to who we are makes us true champions.*

CHAPTER 8

THE LEADER: INSPIRE THROUGH YOUR DREAM

Use love as a bridge.

—GUSTAVO CERATI

#VIRTUOUSCIRCLE

Leaders

BECOME THE CHANGE
THEY WANT TO SEE
IN THE WORLD.

@GABYNATALE

Take a photo and share it online using
#VirtuousCircle

The leader is the seventh and final archetype of *the Virtuous Circle*. The leader comes into your life to put your achievements at the service of something bigger than yourself. The leader inspires, raises awareness, and is an agent of positive change.

Together with the leader you will inspire others by sharing the dream you achieved with the champion, you fought for with the warrior, you perfected with the apprentice, you executed with the maker, you planned with the architect, and you visualized with the dreamer.

The champion and the leader are not equal. The champion achieves triumphs. The leader uplifts.

In politics, business, entertainment, or sports, to name just a few, there are plenty of examples of outstanding people who, despite having accomplished a lot, look after their own interests only. They forget that with greater privilege comes greater responsibility.

When this happens, champions miss their opportunity to become true leaders. Their victories, although great, are reduced to mere collections of individual triumphs. They don't open doors for others' advancement. They are conquerors, not transformers.

Leaders have a guiding principle: to become the change they wish to see in the world.

Leaders are always one step ahead. In times of darkness, their task is to remind us that there is still light. That hope is alive. That our humanity is an invisible thread that unites us all and overcomes any differences we may have with one another.

In times of light, task of leaders is to remind us that darkness still lurks. That the progress made must never be taken for granted. That the sacrifices made were worth it.

Being a leader is not something for the chosen few. *Within each of us lives a potential leader waiting to be released.* To awaken the leader, you need to discover your own light and use it to help others.

You already know the leader. You leader self is the one who guides your steps when you practice what you preach, when you choose to do what is right over what is easy, or when you stand up for the most vulnerable among us. Even without knowing it, you embodied the leader every time you had the courage to defend what is fair, advised a good friend, or gave a word of encouragement to someone whose soul was in pain.

The leader gives you the gift of transcendence. It teaches you that nobody is too small to make an impact on others. Everyone, without exception, has a circle of influence. Maybe we can reach just one person. Maybe it's your family and friends. Maybe you have millions of followers.

The size of the platform doesn't matter. What does matter is that you discover that within you, *you* have the ability to *be* the change. The freedom, the conviction, the creativity, the determination, and the courage you need to transcend are there. You are much more powerful than you think. Under your skin there is *already* unlimited potential to touch the lives of others. Use it.

Prayer for the Time of Decision
Lord, help me to tell the truth to the strong and to avoid telling lies to win the applause of the weak.

If you give me fortune, don't take away my reason.

If you give me success, do not take away my humility.
If you give me humility, do not take away my dignity.

Help me always see the other side of the medal.
Don't let me accuse others of treason for not thinking like me.
Teach me to love people as I love myself
  and not to judge myself as others.

Don't let me be proud if I succeed. Nor fall in despair if I fail.
Remind me that failure is the experience that precedes triumph.

Teach me that forgiveness is the greatest in the strong
and that revenge is the most primitive sign in the weak.

If you take away my success,
  let me keep my strength to overcome failure.
If I fail people, give me courage to apologize.
If people fail me, give me courage to forgive them.
Lord, if I forget you, never forget me.

—APOCRYPHAL PRAYER FREQUENTLY
ATTRIBUTED TO MAHATMA GANDHI

THE LEADER'S MISSION: BEING THE CHANGE

Being the change means becoming a mirror of those qualities you would like to find in the world. Allow your greatness to take control of your life. Let your highest self steer your ship.

Remember that nothing speaks as loudly as our actions. The only true legacy we have is our own life. Transform it into a megaphone by leading by example.

If you want more love in the world, why don't you become an expression of that love? An act of kindness toward a stranger on the street, a surprise call to express your gratitude to someone who feels forgotten, or simply helping those who are at the beginning of a path that you have already traveled—these are simple ways to express the leader that lives in you.

When you walk the leader's path you will notice that you are putting your experience and your achievements at the service of something bigger than yourself. You will experience the satisfaction of going through life with the certainty that you are not only an actor but also an instrument. Don't be afraid of not knowing everything. Let yourself be guided by your intuition. Remember that perfect leaders are not real and real leaders are not perfect.

Wherever you are, you have the opportunity to make a difference. Don't worry about the size of your circle of influence. Those who believe that their impact is too small to leave a mark on this world forget that there is always someone watching us.

Think of the people who had the greatest influence in your life. It is possible that many of them did not have the largest microphone on the planet—but they had the most appropriate message for you.

At home, the leader has a smaller audience but has the most powerful stage of all: everyday life. Family, neighbors, and coworkers share day-to-day life with you. If you have children or siblings, what you do is followed by small pairs of eyes, and they will use you as a role model to decide what to imitate or what to avoid when making their own decisions in the future. Never underestimate your possibility of being an agent of positive change in *the* world and in *your* world.

SOME SUGGESTIONS
TO FEED THE LEADER IN YOU

IF YOU WANT MORE....	IN *YOUR* WORLD	IN *THE* WORLD
...EQUALITY, BECOME AN AGENT IN FAVOR OF EQUALITY	• Be sure to set clear rules in your home so that your children have equal opportunities and obligations. This also applies to household chores. • If the boys are sitting while the girls do all the housework, there is no equality. If the girls assume that boys must pay for everything later on, that's not equal either. • Create a home with zero tolerance for prejudiced comments or jokes against any minority.	• If you have the privilege of moving forward and being in senior management, use it to create changes within your organization that level opportunities for everybody. Don't underestimate the power of leadership that promotes meritocracy and equality. Your section or department must become a role model for the rest. • Raise your voice of opposition when witnessing situations of injustice.

IF YOU WANT MORE....	IN *YOUR* WORLD	IN *THE* WORLD
... EQUALITY, BECOME AN AGENT IN FAVOR OF EQUALITY (*cont.*)	• Choose toys, programs, and entertainment for your children that do not reinforce gender-based stereotypes, such as "boys are only given cars and dolls are only for girls."	• If you hire employees or decide on promotions, make sure you offer equal compensation and growth opportunities to those who are best qualified to do the job, regardless of gender. • Join organizations or campaigns that support equality.
... INCLUSION, BECOME AN AGENT IN FAVOR OF INCLUSION	• How diverse are your friendships? Aim to expand your circle to include people who have a different background, religion, nationality, sexuality, age, ability, or point of view. You will see how your world expands.	• Treat people the way THEY would like to be treated, not the way YOU would like to be treated. This includes avoiding comments and practices that may be offensive to others, such as jokes and generalizations based on the groups they belong to.

IF YOU WANT MORE....	IN *YOUR* WORLD	IN *THE* WORLD
... INCLUSION, BECOME AN AGENT IN FAVOR OF INCLUSION (*cont.*)	• Teach your children the value of appreciating different cultures, customs, and religions. In music, travel, food, and art you will find entertaining ways to do it. • Cultivate in those around you an unprejudiced vision of those families that are made up in a nontraditional way. You have the power to make them feel included.	• Create an environment where diversity is celebrated and empathy is promoted. Be interested in learning more about the challenges faced by groups you may not belong to. What difficulties do those who have a race, religion, sexuality, social class, age, or health condition different from yours suffer? • Support leaders and organizations that make inclusion a priority.

IF YOU WANT MORE....	IN *YOUR* WORLD	IN *THE* WORLD
...COMPASSION, BECOME AN AGENT IN FAVOR OF COMPASSION	• Close your eyes and try to find within yourself the capacity to love so that you may wish the best for someone who has not behaved well with you. • Remember that people do their best from their level of consciousness. Forgive and you will see that it is you who will feel liberated. • Cultivate in your children the capacity for empathy and compassion for those who are most vulnerable, including homeless people, the elderly, and the sick. Every child who develops compassion for others is a child who will not become a bully.	• As a consumer you have great power. You can use your money to buy products from companies that offer decent employment conditions for their factory workers. • Compassion with the planet and with animals begins at home. You can recycle or make changes to your diet to make the world a more sustainable place. You can also avoid watching shows that exploit animals as entertainment.

FROM STEPPING ON PEOPLE TO UNITING THEM: THE LEADERS THE WORLD NEEDS

A CANDLE LOSES NOTHING BY LIGHTING ANOTHER CANDLE.

—ANONYMOUS

For years, it seemed that the only possible model to reach the top was to watch your back and step on other people. From *American Psycho* to *The Devil Wears Prada*, there are plenty of fictional characters with ascending careers and great triumphs built at others' expense. It is a world in which "winners" can reach the top only if knock competitors and adversaries out of the way.

For these "corporate sociopaths" of film, the end always justifies the means. Lying, taking credit for the work of others, or blaming others for their own mistakes are their only tools to succeed. If someone standing between them and their goal is eliminated, it's nothing more than "collateral damage" on the road to success.

These unscrupulous movie characters didn't come from nowhere. They reflect the abuses of power that unfortunately go unpunished in many organizations.

The most worrying thing is that sometimes these "savage winners" are nothing more than the natural result of the implicit rules of the game in their organizations. Sadly, it's the institutions themselves that sometimes pit employees against one another, confident that this will maximize individual performance.

Part of this goes back to the military-style hierarchies that most organizations and companies adopted in the twentieth century.

In that rigid ecosystem, what each boss wanted was ruthlessly enforced. The characteristics considered desirable in a manager were inspired by those of the military. And their priorities were two: (1) exercise control so that none of "those below" rebel, and (2) try to fulfill the orders of "those above" in the hierarchy.

As a result of this scheme, the opinions of those who led the work teams were rarely questioned, and the vision of the "troops" were rarely taken into account. The good news is that the paradigms are shifting. Advances, both technological and in social consciousness, are rapidly turning these archaic organizations and the "corporate psychopaths" who lead them into museum pieces. Power structures in companies are changing, and what comes next are work patterns and organizations where collaboration plays an increasingly important role.

Tomorrow's leaders need to develop the ability to listen and help one another. It's through the exchange of information, and not isolation, that great ideas and innovations emerge.

Leaders who want to move forward and guarantee a future will have to focus their efforts on uniting people, not stepping on them.

Personally, I am convinced that we are living in the best moment in the history of humankind. And it's not because I live in denial, looking at the reality around me with rose-colored glasses. I am well aware that there is still a lot of work to do to have a better world and eliminate the inequalities that exist on our planet. But despite everything, I feel there are many reasons to be optimistic.

The last two hundred years have been the most transformative in history in terms of social and technological change. We went from a world where people lived as slaves and life expectancy was forty years, to one where the majority of the global population lives in a democracy, life expectancy has doubled, and billions of people can communicate with one another through the Internet.

From the women's vote to marriage equality, what seemed utopian a few years ago is now in the realm of the possible.

We live in an imperfect world, but with a collective consciousness noticeably higher than before. The well-meaning—who are the majority—are on the rise. The "savage winners" are in retreat.

The strongest evidence of this progress is that societies are beginning to ask themselves questions never before asked: *What are the employment conditions of the person who manufactured this product? Is my lifestyle beneficial or harmful to the planet? Is it right for animals to be used as entertainment in circuses, bullfights, or hunting grounds?*

All these questions have a common denominator: the certainty that we are interconnected. More and more people understand that you cannot build upon a foundation of others' pain.

At the professional level, for example, we are transitioning toward a model where information flows freely, and the recommendations of clients, colleagues, teammates, and even former collaborators will play a fundamental role. It will no longer be only the boss's opinion or the annual performance evaluation that decide the range of a worker's possible opportunities. In the era of social networks, karma—personal and professional—travels at light speed. Everything good and bad we have done on our journey is increasingly documented and a click away from going public.

It's not only a presidential candidate with an army of skeletons in the closet whose dark past may come to light. The technology is already such that each employee, colleague, or client has the ability to share their evaluation of our performance in the same way that today we can post our criticism of a restaurant or a new movie.

New generations dream less of joining large multinational companies and more about undertaking their own projects. An increasing number of jobs rely less on where the worker lives and more on talent and relationship networks, both real and virtual, that a worker can bring to the table.

Don't fall into the trap of thinking that by becoming a "savage winner" you will go further. Being a scumbag is not only wrong. It's also short-sighted.

It's relationship networks, and not just the relationships with bosses, that will become the key to progress. That is why the choices we make every day with respect to others are more important than ever.

Remember that true leaders not only illuminate, they also inspire others to discover their own light.

A Voice of Authority

Interview with Deepak Chopra

The principle that governs the leader, that of putting one's achievements at the service of others, marked a before and after in the destiny of Deepak Chopra.

From the moment Chopra decided to embrace his truth and share it with the world, his life turned 180 degrees. Putting his knowledge at the service of others brought an unexpected success and abundance to this immigrant doctor of Indian origin who arrived in the United States with twenty-five dollars in his pocket.

But the road to success was not easy. Before becoming the author of books that have set international sales records, and advisor to stars such as Elizabeth Taylor, Michael Jackson, and Lady Gaga, Deepak had to struggle with the prejudices of those who didn't trust someone with a different origin or different ideas.

Conversing with the author Deepak Chopra in his Carlsbad, California, private office. Deepak is the only guest who literally left me speechless.

As soon as he stepped on American soil, Chopra was shocked with his new homeland.

"In the United States I saw that there was a lot of opulence. It was the land of dreams. But there was also racism and intolerance," Deepak confessed to me in his private office at the Chopra Center, where he received us for our interview.

At first, Deepak tried to go the same direction as the rest of the doctors who surrounded him: he finished his residency and opened his own medical office. During those first years in the United States he had not yet incorporated the wellness techniques that catapulted him to global fame.

After opening his own office, Chopra began to have more and more work. He had money, status, and an established career. He had achieved everything that society's standards dictated as the recipe for success and happiness, but he was not happy. He smoked two packs of cigarettes a day.

He lived stressed out and dissatisfied. Something was missing from his life. A purpose.

During a trip to India, he began to go deeper into everything related to transcendental meditation and Ayurvedic medicine. He decided to follow his own heart and start incorporating that new knowledge. First, he incorporated them in his personal life and then in his practice of medicine.

His patients loved the new approach. His colleagues, on the other hand, gave a cold welcome to Chopra's unconventional vision. Deepak felt the medical community turn its back on him.

"The more I tried to convince them of my point of view, the less successful I was in doing so. One day I realized that I was wasting my time," said Deepak.

Although he tried again and again, he could not convince other doctors of the value of alternative medicine. The more he made the case for it, the more resistance he encountered.

"I realized that the biggest fear I had to overcome was the need for approval," the spiritual guru confessed. "It took me a long time to leave it behind."

The approval that Deepak so desperately sought at that time was that of his colleagues. His particular vision of medicine, one that blends ancient Eastern practices with modern Western techniques, was regarded with distrust by the conventional doctors who worked with him at the New Jersey hospital. At that time (the 1970s and 1980s) there were still few who had heard of alternative medicine.

Fatigued, Chopra decided to follow his path and stop trying to get the validation of his colleagues. From then on he would focus only on being true to his vision and sharing knowledge with his patients. To accomplish that goal, he began writing books that would communicate his particular vision of medicine.

The rest is history. His books became so popular that they were translated into more than fifty different languages and became a sensation around the planet. The doors of opportunity, abundance, and purpose opened when Chopra trusted his greatness and shared his knowledge with the world. Freeing himself from the need to seek the approval of others proved to be the key to Deepak's success.

From that moment, he inspired others with his story and his conviction that within each of us lives a sacred spark that we must nurture.

"We all have a divine potential. An infinite potential. We just have to take the time to get in touch with ourselves," he reminds me before saying goodbye.

A Closer Look

Visit www.GabyNatale.com to watch the full half-hour interview with Deepak Chopra. Deepak shares with Gaby:

- His history as an immigrant in the United States.
- Details of his relationship as an advisor to celebrities such as Lady Gaga, Liz Taylor, and Michael Jackson.
- The most important step that must be taken by someone looking to start down the path of personal transformation.
- His best advice for a successful and lasting marriage.

In the First Person

Sharing My Story and Inspiring Others

The tables were already full. Hundreds of people were waiting for the event to begin. Among them, in the front row, the mysterious stranger occupied her seat. Lost in my own thoughts, I didn't notice her. The stage director gave me the cue to stand by. It was my turn to deliver the keynote presentation.

I went onstage, took a deep breath, and began to speak with my heart wide open. I no longer wanted to be safe. I wanted to show myself as I truly was with my successes, my mistakes, and my vulnerable moments.

So, I took the microphone and started talking nonstop. I shared how ashamed and inadequate I felt when I spent a year and a half unemployed right after I graduated from university. I told them about my frustration at the 21 percent unemployment in Argentina, my home country. I recounted the massive protests across the country demanding food and fair living conditions. I described the indignation of finding many of protesters dead in the streets after the rallies. I talked about the despair we felt when we saw five presidents come and go in only ten days. The words flowed effortlessly, and I felt in communion with the audience. From the front row, a pair of female eyes began to pay me special attention.

I confessed that in my lowest moments I spent whole days in pajamas. I was looking for a job without luck, and as the months went by I started to get distressed. I began to mistakenly assume that this lack of results reflected my value as a person. I was trapped in a vicious circle: the more I failed to get results, the more I got depressed, and the more I got depressed, the more difficult it was to get results.

I told them about the day I almost gave up. A friend had called me to offer me a gig for the day as an assistant at a political marketing conference. They had no budget for this position so my salary would be . . . zero. I agreed to do the job, but I felt like a failure. *Why had I studied so much?*

During my presentation at the #*WeAllGrow* conference that takes place every year in California. Without knowing it, this talk would change my life and mark the beginning of a path that would lead me to publish this book you are reading.

To end up moving chairs and handing out flyers without even getting paid? Worst of all was that many of those who graduated in my class and had gotten real jobs in big companies would be attending. They would have front row seats to see firsthand the kind of "total loser" I had transformed myself into.

I thought maybe calling the whole thing off would be the best. Luckily, a conversation with my mother made me reconsider and not cancel my commitment. The next day, I went to work with my best attitude even if I didn't receive a penny for my work.

That day I almost gave up turned out to be the day that changed my luck. Last minute, the translator hired by the event organizers called in sick, and I was assigned as his replacement. My newly assigned job was to interpret for a delegation of professors who came from the United States. Those professors were the ones who took a chance on me and started giving me remote assignments. Eventually those remote assignments became an offer to join their team full time in Washington, D.C. It was a great life lesson.

I could sense from the stage that people identified with my many of my struggles. I followed the voice of enthusiasm, threw the "what will they say" out the window, and spoke bluntly. Sharing my story was the best thing I could have done!

Before saying goodbye, I left the advice my mom always offered in times of crisis: "Always bring your A game because you never know when opportunity will knock on your door." I stepped off the stage without imagining how prophetic that advice from Mama Cristina would be.

The audience connected with the message and the speech was a success. In the first row, the stranger had already made a decision.

Tick . . . the circle closed.

The next day, I took my flight back home. I flew with my heart happy to have faced my fears and to have followed the voice of enthusiasm. I gave myself credit for being able to savor the moment, no matter the results.

Days later, I received a letter that made my jaw drop. A woman who had been among the #WeAllGrow audience had been particularly moved by my story. The "stranger" in the front row, who had flown from the other side of the country to attend the Storytellers gala, was named Aleyso and was a literary agent. She wanted to represent me and work together to turn my message into a book.

We met in Miami to finalize the details and get to know each other. I told her that I had compiled interviews, personal stories, and material for decades to create a manual of personal transformation. I already had everything thought out for the book . . . even the title. We just needed to meet!

Three months later, *The Virtuous Circle* already had publishing offers. I would never have thought that fate would so generously reward the small act of courage of that year-end exercise I wrote about in the introduction. That was the seed of the book you are reading today.

This book also made its own turn in *the Virtuous Circle*. I visualized it sitting in the yard of my house with a notebook in hand, like any *dreamer*. As an *architect*, I planned the structure and messages of each chapter. The *maker* in me spent months writing, while the *apprentice* looked through it and asked me to do some rewrites to fine tune the chapters when something did not convince her.

My internal *warrior* was the one who persevered in those hours when the blank computer screen greeted me and the muses were conspicuous by their absence. And when the preparation, the desire, and the opportunity aligned, the *champion* emerged, finding herself on her way with a publishing house that gave the project a green light.

Finally, it was the *leader* in me who demanded that I share my path and inspire others, leaving aside fears and shame so that this book honestly shares what I experienced in the hopes it can be useful to someone else.

When I received confirmation that this book was finally going to be published, I got excited. I remembered all my fears before I sent that video to enter the *#WeAllGrow* contest. And I thought of those two voices, fear and enthusiasm, that dueled in my heart and my mind.

At that moment, I remembered one of my favorite fables: the Cherokee legend of the two wolves. The tale goes like this:

One morning, an old Cherokee told his grandson about a battle that takes place inside all people.

"My son, in each of us live two wolves who are fighting to the death," he said. "One is evil: it is the wolf of fear, anger, envy, jealousy, sadness, sorrow, greed, arrogance, self-pity, guilt, resentment, pride, inferiority, lies, false pride, superiority, and ego."

And then he continued:

"The other wolf is good: it is the wolf of enthusiasm, joy, peace, love, hope, serenity, humility, kindness, benevolence, friendship, empathy, generosity, truth, compassion, and faith."

The grandson pondered for a minute and then asked:

"Which wolf is the winner?"

"The one you feed," replied the wise old Cherokee.

This is what the speakers' presentation cards looked like at the *#WeAllGrow* conference.

Conclusion

FROM *THE VIRTUOUS CIRCLE* TO THE VIRTUOUS SPIRAL

Lie down and fall asleep to wake up
Smiling and happy
Wake up, get up to get tired
And go back to sleep
The circle goes around
And when it's finished, it goes around again . . .[1]

—KEVIN JOHANSEN

#VᴵʀᴛᴜᴏᴜsCᴵʀᴄʟᴇ

WHAT YOU
ARE LOOKING FOR
is already in you.
SET IT FREE.

@Gᴀʙʏ Nᴀᴛᴀʟᴇ

Take a photo and share it online using
#VirtuousCircle

We have the ability to be our own best friend or our worst enemy. The saboteur and the advocate live both within us. At the end of the day, the choice is ours. The time we have left on the planet will pass anyway regardless of our decision. But one thing is certain: we did not come to this world to travel it as a diminished version of ourselves. Our mission is to find our light, make it shine, and share it with others.

The Virtuous Circle teaches us that greatness is already within our being. It's our natural state. We are the ones stopping it from coming forth by clinging to prejudices, insecurities, and fears. Our job is to remove all these things that harm us, layer by layer, in order to become the best version of ourselves. For that:

- Visualize what you have to visualize.
- Plan what you have to plan.
- Execute what you have to execute.
- Perfect what you have to perfect.
- Persevere in what you have to persevere.
- Achieve what you have to achieve.
- Inspire what you have to inspire.

And when you're done going around *the Virtuous Circle*, start over. Make your life a *Virtuous Spiral* where the dreamer in you becomes a leader by sharing your light . . . and where your leader self becomes a dreamer again when facing each new goal or challenge.

Change is the only constant in our evolution. Every beginning is followed by an end. Every end, by a beginning.

Remember that when you open yourself up to the world, the world opens itself up to you. That's why it's important that you start right now. Start your personal revolution. Take that leap of faith. Don't let anyone but yourself define your potential.

For me, writing this book also meant going around *the Virtuous Circle*. There are many things in my life at the moment that feel like new cycles ready to begin, while others are being fulfilled. I write these last lines completing a lap that comes to an end. And I give this book to the world to do with it what it wants.

Meanwhile, I embark on the humble path of starting another lap in my own spiral destiny. I put myself in the arms of the dreamer, embrace the unknown, and start visualizing the next horizons of this adventure that is life. *May the Virtuous Circle guide my steps.*

I say goodbye with these lines I hope will soothe your soul and encourage you to continue trusting your greatness even in times of turbulence.

When you can't find your way and you feel surrounded by fog, return to *The Virtuous Circle.*

In times of hopelessness,
Visualize and become a dreamer again.
In times of chaos,
Plan and become an architect again.
In times of stagnation,
Execute and become a maker again.
In times of decline,
Perfect and become an apprentice again.
In times of weakness,
Persevere and become a warrior again.
In times of defeat,
Honor your achievements and become a champion again.
In times of meanness,
Inspire (sharing what you know) and become a leader again.

Nurture the Virtuous Circle. Trust the Virtuous Circle. Let yourself be guided by the Virtuous Circle.

And never forget that what you are looking for is already in you. Release it.

—Gaby Natale

At the close
of this edition . . .

. . . Gaby Natale won her third Daytime Emmy award, becoming the first television host in the United States to win the Best Talent in a Spanish-Language Program award two years in a row.

In her acceptance speech, Gaby dedicated her prize to the beauty of diversity, because she never forgot that big dreams can start in unusual places . . . like a carpet warehouse.

Acknowledgments

This book would not exist if it weren't for a long list of people who, throughout my life and my career, have helped me selflessly, without expecting anything in return. Here are my incomplete thanks in more or less chronological order.

First of all, I thank my parents, Roberto Natale and María Cristina Camelino, for giving me a beautiful childhood, two brothers that I love, Francisco and Alejandro, and the freedom to discover myself in my choices, to learn from my mistakes, and grow to smile and stumble. Thank you both for sharing your views as readers to enrich the manuscript.

To my great love, Andy Suarez. Thank you for the rereadings, for the unlimited yerba mate teas you prepared during the writing of the book, for the patience in the face of my almost monothematic conversations for months about *The Virtuous Circle*, but fundamentally thanks for being my amazing companion in good times and bad. Walking this adventure-filled road by your side has been the most beautiful thing that has happened to me in life.

My thanks to my family, aunts, uncles, cousins, and grandparents who give me love from this and other dimensions. My deepest thanks go to my friends from La Plata—Carolina, Florencia, Valeria, Catiana, Lucía and Silvina, and from Buenos Aires, Paula, Natalia, María, and the always present Lucecita Bonadeo—for giving me their company in person and from a distance for decades now. Thanks to Martita and the Suarez-Benitez family for accompanying this process with all their love.

Thanks to those who gave me that first opportunity to come to work in the United States, to Azteca television in Hermosillo, Sonora, for giving me my first opportunity to work in front of the camera in Aztec land. I also thank the entire KUPB Univision West Texas team for my first full-time job as a reporter.

Most especially, I thank Barry Marks, then general manager of CBS 7, for offering us a space on MyTV16 in West Texas and a carpet warehouse to create our first *SuperLatina* show. Together with Barry, I also want to recognize John Bushman, José, Kathy, Elías Hernández, Martin Gonzalez, and so many people from CBS and ICA who offered us their support from, literally, the beginning of this adventure called *SuperLatina*.

To Telemundo KWES and its management (thanks for the warmth and companionship of Patsy Casas and Luis Carlos!). And since we are in West Texas, I don't want to forget to mention the MCH team with Jacqui Gore at the head and that of the Small Business Administration of Odessa for helping us with our first business plan, and Andy Espinoza, of the American State Bank, for approval of our first loan to start *SuperLatina*.

Many thanks to Manuel Abud of Telemundo Dallas and Miguel Villegas and the entire Azteca Dallas team for helping us with the growth of *SuperLatina*, and the tireless Ana Ruedaquinteiro and Doris Vogelmann of VME TV and their boss, Eligio Cedeño, for realizing our dream of transforming that little show that began in an Odessa carpet warehouse into a show that is seen all over the country today and has won three Emmys.

To La Gran Plaza of Fort Worth and Miguel Calera, thank you for so many years of accompanying and supporting our growth in the Latino community. Thanks to Paulina Magdaleno and all our dear #Team*SuperLatina* now and always including Ana Cruz, Oscar Fierro, Leslie Rodriguez, Mayde, Jaime, Leo D'Almagro, and Adriana Lopez.

My deepest thanks go to Manny and Angela Ruiz, along with the entire Hispanicize team, for all the connections and good advice over the years, and also especially to Ana Flores and her #*WeAll-Grow* association for giving me the opportunity of sharing my story on the stage of your conference. Not to mention the person who in that #*WeAllGrow* conference heard that story and believed in my ability to create this book you have in your hands today.

Aleyso Bridger, thank you for trusting me and seeing something that not even I had discovered, and thanks for connecting me with the wonderful people of Spanish HarperCollins, Edward Benitez and Graciela Lelli, whose support and direction were invaluable. Thank you for trusting my vision and giving me the possibility of having my first book published.

My deepest gratitude to HarperCollins Leadership and Sara Kendrick for trusting in *The Virtuous Circle*, bringing this book to global audiences and allowing me the great honor of becoming the first Latina author to be signed by this division of HarperCollins.

Finally, I want to thank God for giving me the strength and clarity to pursue my dream, to my native country, Argentina, for teaching me the value of critical thinking and irreverence, and to my adopted country, the United States, for showing me that it is still the land of dreams and opportunities.

Notes

Chapter 2

1. John Stuart Mill, *On Liberty* (Ebook, 2014), 110, http://www.gutenberg.org/files/34901/34901-h/34901-h.htm.

Chapter 3

1. Amado Nervo, "At Peace," trans. Dave Bonta, Via Negativa, https://www.vianegativa.us/2015/06/eternity-for-an-inheritance-eight-poems-by-amado-nervo/

Chapter 4

1. *Mijita* (pronounced me-he-taah) is used affectionately as shorthand for "*mi hijita*," or "my daughter," in Spanish.
2. Kent Keith, *The Paradoxical Commandments: How to Find Personal Meaning in a Crazy World* (Madrid: Editorial Topics of Today, 2002), https://www.paradoxicalcommandments.com.
3. *Abu* is short for *abuela*, which means "grandmother" in Spanish.

Chapter 5

1. Will Durant, *The Story of Philosophy* (New York: Simon and Schuster, 1926), 61. The author is paraphrasing Aristotle.
2. *Nagual* (pronounced nuh-guh-al) is a physical and/or spiritual healer. *Nagual* and *nahual* are two forms of the Toltec word for "someone with healing powers and abilities."

3. *Quinceañera* is a rite of passage for fifteen-year-old Latina girls, as they make their transition from childhood to womanhood. Similar to a Sweet Sixteen. *Quinceañeras* are what the celebrants are called.

Conclusion

1. Translated from Spanish. Kevin Johansen, "El circulo" [The circle], *The Nada* (Buenos Aires: Warner Chappell Music Argentina, 2000).